Ethics and Academic Freedom in Educational Research

Formal ethical review of research proposals is now almost the default requirement for all – staff and students – planning research under the auspices of colleges and universities in many parts of the world. With notable exceptions, the extant literature discussing educational research ethics takes a meta-ethical overview, is negatively critical about the ethics review process per se, or comes from America and focuses specifically on the workings of the Institutional Review Boards (IRBs) there.

This book, however, contains stories of lived experience from the UK, Spain, New Zealand, Bangladesh, and Australia, dealing with inter alia: dissatisfactions with criteria against which research proposals and designs and, by extension, researchers themselves are judged to be ethical; problems encountered in obtaining ethical clearance; changes which have had to be made to plans which are believed to have affected the ensuing research process and outcomes; cases where ethical issues and difficulties arose and required considered responses despite permission to undertake the research in question being granted; and benefits perceived to accrue from ethical review procedures.

Ethics and Academic Freedom in Educational Research will be of interest to researchers, students, members of ethics review boards and those teaching research ethics, primarily at postgraduate but also at undergraduate level.

This book was originally published as a special issue of the *International Journal of Research & Method in Education.*

Pat Sikes is Professor of Qualitative Inquiry at the University of Sheffield, UK.

Heather Piper is a Professorial Research Fellow within the Education and Social Research Institute (ESRI) at Manchester Metropolitan University, UK.

I0895461

Ethics and Academic Freedom in Educational Research

Edited by
Pat Sikes and Heather Piper

Routledge
Taylor & Francis Group
LONDON AND NEW YORK

First published 2011
by Routledge
2 Park Square, Milton Park, Abingdon, Oxfordshire OX14 4RN

Simultaneously published in the USA and Canada
by Routledge
711 Third Avenue, New York, NY 10017

First issued in paperback 2014

Routledge is an imprint of the Taylor and Francis Group, an informa company

This book is a reproduction of the *International Journal of Research & Method in Education*, volume 33, issue 3. The Publisher requests to those authors who may be citing this book to state, also, the bibliographical details of the special issue on which the book was based.

British Library Cataloguing in Publication Data
A catalogue record for this book is available from the British Library

ISBN13: 978-0-415-66921-4 (hbk)
ISBN13: 978-0-415-75467-5 (pbk)

Typeset in Times New Roman
by Taylor & Francis Books

Disclaimer
The publisher would like to make readers aware that the chapters in this book are referred to as articles as they had been in the special issue. The publisher accepts responsibility for any inconsistencies that may have arisen in the course of preparing this volume for print.

Contents

Notes on contributors

Patrick Carmichael is a Professor of Educational Research, at the Faculty of Education, Community and Leisure, Liverpool John Moores University, UK.

Rosemary De Luca is Chair of University of Waikato Human Research Ethics Committee and a Lecturer in the Department of Professional Studies, University of Waikato, New Zealand.

Renée DePalma is a Lecturer in the Facultade de Ciencias da Educación, University of Vigo, Spain.

Tanya Fitzgerald is Professor of Educational Leadership and Management at the Faculty of Education, La Trobe University, Australia.

Lariane Fonseca is an Academic Development Advisor for the Faculty of Life and Social Sciences at Swinburne Professional Learning, Swinburne University of Technology, Australia.

M. Obaidul Hamid is a Lecturer in Education at the School of Education, The University of Queensland, Australia.

John O'Neill is Professor of Teacher Education at the School of Arts, Development and Health Education, Massey University, New Zealand.

Heather Piper is a Professorial Research Fellow within the Education and Social Research Institute (ESRI), at Manchester Metropolitan University, UK.

Clive C. Pope is a Professor in the Department of Sport & Leisure Studies, University of Waikato, New Zealand.

Catherine Lomas Scott is a Senior Research Fellow on the Teaching, Learning and Leadership Program, Australian Council for Educational Research, Camberwell, Australia.

Pat Sikes is Professor of Qualitative Inquiry at the University of Sheffield, UK.

Martin Tolich is an Associate Professor in the Department of Anthropology, Gender & Sociology, University of Otago, New Zealand.

Frances Tracy is a Research Associate in the Faculty of Education, Community and Leisure, at Liverpool John Moores University, UK.

Julie White is a Senior Lecturer at the Faculty of Education, La Trobe University, Australia.

Notes on contributors

Ethical research, academic freedom and the role of ethics committees and review procedures in educational research

Introduction

Our aim is to re-present and reflect educational researchers' lived experiences of ethical review committees and procedures. We decided to put together this collection as a result of what happened to us when we sought clearance for an undoubtedly sensitive study of the perceptions and experiences of male schoolteachers (and those of members of their families, their friends and colleagues) accused of sexual misconduct with female students which they said they had not committed and of which they were eventually cleared or where the case was dismissed (Sikes and Piper 2008, 2010). We had a difficult time and consequently became curious about how it was for others. However, with notable exceptions such as Burgess (1984), Nind et al. (2005) and Simons and Usher (2000) the available literature concerning educational research ethics largely took a meta-ethical overview, or was negatively critical about the ethics review process *per se*, or came from America and focused specifically on the workings of the Institutional Review Boards (IRBs) in that country. We, therefore, decided to investigate whether and to what extent Mark Israel and Iain Hay's claim that:

> social scientists are angry and frustrated. They believe their work is being constrained and distorted by regulators of ethical practice who do not understand social science research. In the United States, Canada, the United Kingdom, New Zealand and Australia, researchers have argued that regulators are acting on the basis of biomedically driven arrangements that make little or no sense to social scientists. (2006, 1)

spoke to the contemporary experience of educational researchers. Thus, we solicited, stories dealing with, *inter alia*: dissatisfactions with criteria against which research proposals and designs and, by extension, researchers themselves, are judged to be ethical; problems encountered in obtaining ethical clearance; changes (of whatever kind) which have had to be made in order to be allowed to proceed and how these are believed to have affected the ensuing research (positively or negatively); cases where ethical issues and difficulties arose despite permission to undertake the research in question being granted; and, the benefits perceived to accrue from more stringent and closer control of research practice consequent on ethical review procedures. We are also sought stories of satisfaction and accounts where the ethical review process did have positive outcomes.

This call, with its emphasis on personal experience, clearly struck a chord for we received over 50 enquiries, primarily, but not exclusively, from the countries Israel and Hay mentioned. Perhaps inevitably, given both the wording of the call and the propensity of people to feel moved to complain about bad experiences rather than to praise good ones, the majority of responses concerned troubles, disagreements, barriers and prohibitions. We had, however, asked for positive accounts as well and a number of these were forthcoming, albeit usually offered by those who had an official role in the ethics review process.

Historical developments and their consequences

Within the social sciences generally, and education in particular, the requirement to subject research proposals to ethical scrutiny by a formally constituted body is a relatively recent development. Histories of the development of ethics review procedures usually trace a line from the Nuremberg Nazi war crimes trials (Mitscherliche and Mielke 1947) through the *Tuskegee Study of Untreated Syphilis in the Negro Male* (Jones 1981) and, (if UK based), the *Alder Hey Organ Retention* case (Redfern 2001). Thus, medical scandals and the moral panics they generate are credited with being the impetus for the institution of regulatory systems of ethical oversight. Having originally been established in order to deal with biomedical research which obviously can, in some cases, involve the possibility of very serious harm being done to research participants, it would seem that the model has tended to prevail, pervade and persist, coming also to be applied to research in the social sciences, the arts and the humanities where research is rarely life threatening. Subsequently in America, the 1990s saw a growth in the scope and influence of IRBs (Institutional Review Boards), heralding what Patricia Adler and Peter Adler have called the 'Dark Ages' (1998, xiv–v) for ethnography in particular.

There is a common saying that what happens in America today affects everywhere else tomorrow and it would certainly seem to be the case that ethical regulation is now experienced by researchers throughout the world and in most disciplines. There has been what Kevin Haggarty describes as 'ethics creep':

> characterized by a dual process whereby the regulatory system is expanding outward to incorporate a host of new activities and institutions, while at the same time intensifying the regulation of activities deemed to fall within its ambit. (2004, 391)

On the basis both of the extant literature, and of what those responding to our call reported, the consequences and the experience tend not to be positive. However, as Israel and Hay point out:

> It is disturbing and not a little ironic that regulators and social scientists find themselves in [a] situation of division, mistrust and antagonism. After all, we each start from the same point: that is, that ethics matter. (2006, 1)

In the UK, Martyn Hammersley is of a similar opinion, and in commenting on the introduction in 2006 of the requirement of the Economic and Social Research Council (ESRC) that its grant holders abide by its ethics framework (ESRC 2005) (described by Saville Kushner as a 'step change in the politics of social research' [2006, 9]), he points out that there is no evidence to suggest that there is or has been 'substantial unethical behaviour on the part of social scientists which would justify such a lack of trust' (Hammersley 2009, 217–18). Indeed, the ESRC themselves have said that 'almost without exception, social science research in the UK has been carried out to high ethical standards' (2005, 1). Examples of social science research which have been considered by some to be unethical, for instance and probably most notably,

Laud Humphreys' (1970) *Tearoom Trade* and Stanley Milgram's (1974) *Obedience to Authority* studies, are relatively rare and in any case, usually raise questions about the difficulties inherent in applying blanket codes to attempts to study aspects of social life where, as Bruce Macfarlane has put it, 'developing an understanding of what to do is always a more challenging prospect than issuing edicts about what is not right' (2009, 3).

Areas of concern

So what are the problems with, and criticisms of, ethical review procedures? Although such procedures do offer a means of opening up research plans to wider view and authoritative discussion which can act as a safeguard for the well-being of those touched by any particular project, they can be viewed as acting in a manner that is antithetical to both ethical research practice and the exercise of academic freedom. As Catherine Scott puts it:

> The rationale for their establishment and continuing development is the prevention of harm. However, this intent to protect has arguably become a license to harm via its ability to prevent research, silence debate, and stymie the acquisition of knowledge about difficult issues. (2008, 13)

It has been suggested (e.g. by Cannella and Lincoln 2007; Halse and Honey 2007; Tierney and Blumberg Corwin 2007; Sikes 2008; Sikes and Piper 2008) that ethics committees are not simply concerned with addressing ethical matters, but now have a tendency to act as gatekeepers, with their chief concern being the avoidance of controversy and litigation. This is, perhaps, almost an inevitable consequence of living within a 'risk' culture (see Beck 1992; Furedi 2002; Castell 1999) where individuals, institutions and organizations seek to manage risk (Power 2004), even when perceived and imagined risks far outweigh the real likelihood of that which is feared, actually happening (Pieterman 2001). In such a culture, ethical review committees, their procedures and the discourses they have developed and promulgated both determine what constitutes ethical research and what ethical researchers do. They can create an 'illusion' of ethical practice which is not necessarily underpinned by a genuine 'philosophical concern for equity and the imposition of power within the conceptualization and practice of research itself' (Cannella and Lincoln 2007, 315). Rather, they work to limit, control and even stop particular research from being done and particular areas of enquiry being explored with inevitable consequences for the exercise of academic freedom.

Issues and areas around ethics review procedures which have attracted particular critique include:

- The establishment of ethics committees based on biomedical models which are governed by principles of scientific, objective, experimental inquiry (see Department of Health's UK 'Research Governance Framework' 2001, revised 2005). These models are problematic enough within their own fields and are often simply inappropriate when used within social contexts which are complex, changing and subject to multiple interpretations (Richardson and McMullan 2007).
- There is by no means consensus concerning which types of ethics should prevail in any particular case. Thus, ethics reviewers may, variously, look at proposals

from a Kantian deontological, a consequentialist, an Aristotelian virtue, a situational or a Buberian relational ethical perspective. Different decisions can hinge on particular viewpoints.

- Membership of ethics review committees can be problematic in that those being required to make judgements may not be experienced in the particular area under consideration. In some cases there is a requirement that certain sectors (e.g. religion, law) be represented and these people may have little or no research experience. It is worth pointing out here that across the world, ethics review is approached in different ways ranging from tightly structured committees through relatively informal procedures.
- The assumption by many ethics review committees of an essentialized view of human beings and human nature, which is manifested by a technicist, one-size-fits-all and once and for all approach. As Richard Pring (2000) points out, each research situation generates its own ethical questions and issues that demand unique and contextual attention on a case-by-case basis (see also Piper and Stronach 2008; Allen et al. 2009). Throughout the course of a research project too, things may change and there may be need for reassessment of ethical risk and concerns.
- A lack of sensitivity to different cultural contexts (Tuhiwai Smith 1999; Cannella and Viruru 2004; Allen et al. 2009).
- The universal and uncritical implementation of consent forms can, as Michelle Fine et al. (2000) (amongst others) note, be invoked to absolve researchers from their moral and ethical responsibilities. Furthermore, what Scott (2003, 2008) depicts as the contemporary 'obsession' with consent forms also infantilizes research participants and especially those considered 'vulnerable', such as children and babies, the differently abled and indigenous peoples. Ironically, the wordy and detailed character of many consent forms means that they may well conceal more than they reveal (Scott 2008, 18). In addition, consent forms are not sensitive to contexts and cultures where signing one's name can cause unease, suspicion and even fear (e.g. Tuhiwai Smith 1999; Bristol 2008; Redwood 2008).
- While potentially infantilizing research participants, ethics review committees cast researchers as irresponsible, dangerous (Sikes and Piper 2008) and even as 'morons' (Tierney and Blumberg Corwin 2007, 396) against whom people need protecting. This carries risks of de-motivation and de-professionalization (see Piper and Stronach 2008).
- Ethics review committees can enforce methodological conservatism (Lincoln 2005; Johnson 2008a), especially when there is already a tendency, if not a stronger imperative, for researchers to use particular approaches if they wish their work to attract official approbation or funding.
- Ethics review committees may be cautious about granting permission for research on 'difficult' or 'sensitive' topics, for example those which link children/young people and sex (e.g. Piper and Stronach 2008; Sikes 2008; Sikes and Piper 2008; Johnson 2008b), or which involve people deemed by the members of the committee to be 'vulnerable' (e.g. parents of terminally ill children [Redwood 2008]: young people diagnosed with eating disorders and their parents [Halse and Honey 2007]). The consequence of this is that attempts to expand knowledge which might be used to address the problems under investigation are felled at the first hurdle.

Between them, the accounts in this collection address all of the above concerns. We must stress that the brief we gave to authors asked for lived experience. Thus, the accounts describe how the authors interpreted and made sense of what happened to them and are, therefore, situational and specific. What they all make clear is the way in which zeitgeist, politics, organizational reform and legislation at the national and local level all impact upon the ethics review process by affecting understandings about what is and is not ethical or what is, or is not, potentially risky research.

Introducing the content

Renée DePalma describes some of the ethical issues involved in an ESRC-funded project which investigated approaches to lesbian, gay, bisexual and transgender equalities in primary schools in England. Interestingly this project, despite its seemingly 'risky' research focus, appeared to experience very little difficulty in gaining initial ethical approval. However, the author describes how the ethical thinking and practice involved in negotiating consent and safety, for example, emerged throughout the two-and-a-half year process within the research community. Some of the decisions made at the initial ethical clearance stage especially in relation to anonymity, served the needs of the lead university in terms of protecting it against litigation, and in fact silenced the voices of those with less capital within the project (those in schools rather than universities) which in effect restricted their agency. The process of ethical thinking and practice shares some similarities with other accounts in describing both the ongoing nature of ethical thinking and in something akin to the contextual development of ethical wisdom.

John O'Neill writes from the vantage point of being a long-standing member (including being a chair, and now the director of research ethics with a personal agenda to 'serve') of an ethics committee in Massey University, New Zealand. This piece is the only one in the collection which required ethics approval for gathering the data to support its writing and it offers an interesting insight into the workings of one committee. It also serves to provide a setting in which to consider many of the issues raised by ourselves and the other authors. For instance, it describes why applications may be initially rejected, and it admits to the lack of expertise in relation to educational and some social science research of many members of the committee. However, of even greater significance perhaps – the account is written from the implicit assumption that ethics approval is a process that precedes the research activity. It is therefore something which can be anticipated in advance. Most of the other authors writing here dispute this assumption.

Frances Tracy and Patrick Carmichael offer some tensions that emerged during a participatory research project in an interdisciplinary technology-focussed study. Again they discuss the necessary ongoing nature of ethical practice and offers the idea of 'phronesis' and 'practical wisdom' with its Aristotelian roots which necessarily rejects the Kantian, deontological perspective. This story highlights the challenges that can arise in interdisciplinary team work.

Obdaidul Hamid writes from the experience of carrying out research in Bangladesh for his PhD whilst having to satisfy the ethics committee of an Australian university. He provides an interesting account of how the forms and process were not fit for purpose in the context where he carried out his research. The author describes how the committee did not like his 'over wordy' documentation prepared to hand out to various authorities even though he knew that 'over wordy' was expected and the norm.

Informed consent is a particular interesting aspect of this contribution, and the description that for someone not to be invited to be a research participant was considered a slight, and that informed consent of young people was wholly inappropriate in a setting where all were proud to be part of the process, and good manners include doing what adults ask of you, especially academics. This story clearly demonstrates the inappropriateness of one set of cultural norms imposing so-called 'ethical' standards on another – which when considered through a different lens, seem anything but ethical.

From a slightly different angle, Julie White and Tanya Fitzgerald each provide a 'tale' to support their desire for a more 'continuing narrative approach' to ethical research. Julie offers a tale of research which included meeting Lanie who is from a Chinese background and who has an eating disorder. Eventually it emerges that she has virtually been imprisoned and force-fed (actually hospitalized and given no choice – and with the blessing of her parents) for a period of four months, in a Chinese psychiatric institution. Julie worried about her responsibilities and found this distressing and eventually spoke with an ethicist. The ethicist reassured her that she was a researcher 'and had no business involving myself in psychological and medical aspects of this youngster's life'. This raises interesting ethical issues: (1) in relation to someone presumably from one cultural background (Australian?) carrying out research with someone from another (Chinese background) which brings into play some of the issues raised above, but also (2) what are a researcher's moral (and legal) responsibilities in relation to children presumably living in the same country as the researcher (in this case Australia)? While we have little knowledge of Australian legislation, in the UK 'Under The Children Act 1989, all adults who work with young people have a legal responsibility to report sexual (and physical) abuse to the appropriate authority. Social (and other) researchers are not exempt from such a legal requirement' (France et al. 2000, 160). It is arguable that the regime endured by Lanie, as described, would constitute abuse in an Australian institution – and maybe a different ethicist would have reached a different conclusion, which again raises issues of who is qualified to be an ethicist and in what contexts? Tanya describes working with a group of Maori women, which involves issues of power and negotiation, and some of her experience mirrors that of Hamid above.

Catherine Scott and Lariane Fonseca also write from an Australian perspective. They offer a more critical view of the motives and actions of ethical committees to the extent of suggesting that committees who appear to have set themselves up as 'enemies' of researchers could be described as a psychiatric symptom perhaps reflective of other difficulties experienced by universities in difficult times. They describe a number of examples including problems encountered when carrying out research requiring a 'visual' component (e.g. videos, photos, etc.), and explain how one of them had to change the nature of their planned project entirely as everyone in a very old photograph could not be contacted to give their permission for its inclusion in a PhD thesis. As they explain, those of us in the West are under constant surveillance of one sort or another and this level of sensitivity could seem absurd. There is a further point we add here in relation to the distortion of images and pixilating faces, and only showing legs of children in a playground (which is common on UK news reports at least), i.e. showing part for whole (leg for child, bottom for baby in nappy adverts) makes fetishisms of these parts in the same way that a stiletto shoe is supposed to provide a fetish relating to a sexual woman. Distorting children's images in this way is most likely feeding into the problem it assumes it is dealing with – instead new fetishes are created around the very young.

This problem with the visual image is also picked up in Clive Pope's, Rosemary De Luca's and Martin Tolich's writing from the context in New Zealand. Their account partly consists of a dialogue between a researcher, a member of the relevant ethics committee and an informed outsider who discuss the process of gaining ethics approval for a particular project. A number of issues are raised with both the researcher and ethics committee learning from the experience. Such a three-way dialogue offers a unique insight into one particular instance of decision making.

Finally

We think that it is reasonable to assume that few, if any, researchers set out with a deliberate intention to bring about harm. We acknowledge that sometimes researchers may be too 'close' to their work to look at it with sufficient dispassion or that they may fail to spot the potential for unintended consequences. We suspect that the vast majority of applications for ethics review are passed with no or very minor amendments. However, we do take the view that, as they are presently constituted, many ethics review policies and procedures are potentially measures of governance and regulation, affecting the sorts of research that is or is not done, the issues that are or are not investigated, and simply fail to take the realities of lived experience in to account. In recent years more and more people have begun to question the role of ethics review as currently constituted and it is probably fair to say that, in some institutions, much time and effort is being put into working towards developing approaches to ethical oversight which address issues such as the way in which research projects evolve making once and for all ethical approval inappropriate. Similarly, growing numbers of students from around the world have focused attention on the need to be aware of the ways in which imposition of western ethics requirements do not always meet local conditions and can be experienced as yet another example of colonization. Issues around research ethics will not go away and as new technologies become available and are used in research, more and more questions will arise (and we acknowledge that here we have no examples of internet or virtual research). It seems to us that the best way forward is to examine examples of lived experience of ethics review in order to see what we can learn from them. This collection is a contribution to that endeavour.

Acknowledgement

We would like to thank Geoffrey Walford for his help with this edition.

References

Adler, P., and P. Adler. 1998. Foreword: Moving backward. In *Ethnography at the edge: Crime, deviance and field research,* ed. J. Ferrell and M. Hamm, xiii–xvi. New Hampshire: North-eastern University Press.

Allen, A., K. Anderson, L. Bristol, Y. Downs, D. O'Neill, N. Watts, and Q. Wu. 2009. Resisting the unethical in formalised ethics: Perspectives and experiences. In *Power in the academy,* ed. J. Satterthwaite, H. Piper, and P. Sikes, 135–52. Stoke-on-Trent: Trentham Books.

Beck, U. 1992. *Risk society: Towards a new modernity.* London: Sage.

Bristol, L. 2008. Ethics review committees: A decolonising perspective. Paper presented at the DPR conference, March 18–20, Manchester Metropolitan University.

Burgess, R.G. 1984. *In the field: An introduction to field research.* London: Allen & Unwin.

Cannella, G., and Y. Lincoln. 2007. Predatory vs dialogic ethics: Constructing an illusion or ethical practice as the core of research methods. *Qualitative Inquiry* 13, no. 3: 315–35.

Cannella, G., and R. Viruru. 2004. *Childhood and postcolonization: Power, education and contemporary practice.* New York: Routledge/Falmer.

Castell, R. 1999. From dangerousness to risk. In *The Foucault effect: Studies in governmentality,* ed. G. Burchell, C. Gordon, and P. Miller, 281–98. Chicago, IL: University of Chicago Press.

Department of Health. 2005. *Research governance framework: Second edition.* http://www.dh.gov.uk/en/Publicationsandstatistics/Publications/PublicationsPolicyAndGuidance/DH_4108962 (accessed July 7, 2010).

ESRC (Economic and Social Research Council). 2005. *Research ethics framework.* http://www.esrc.ac.uk/ESRCInfoCentre/Images/ESRC_Re_Ethics_Frame_tcm6-11291.pdf (accessed July 7, 2010).

Fine, M., L. Weiss, S. Wessen, and L. Wong. 2000. For whom? Qualitative research, representations and social responsibilities. In *The handbook of qualitative research,* ed. N. Denzin and Y. Lincoln, 2nd ed., 107–31. Thousand Oaks, CA: Sage.

France, A., G. Bendelow, and S. Williams. 2000. A 'risky' business: researching the health beliefs of children and young people. In *Researching Children's perspectives,* ed. A. Lewis and G. Lindsay, 150–162. Buckingham: Open University.

Furedi, F. 2002. *The culture of fear: Risk-taking and the morality of low expectation.* 2nd ed. London: Continuum.

Haggarty, K.D. 2004. Ethics creep: Governing social science research in the name of ethics. *Qualitative Sociology* 27, no. 4: 391–414.

Halse, C., and A. Honey. 2007. Rethinking ethics review as institutional discourse. *Qualitative Inquiry* 13, no. 3: 336–52.

Hammersley, M. 2009. Against the ethicists: On the evils of ethical regulation. *International Journal of Social Research Methodology* 12, no. 3: 217–18.

Humphreys, L. 1970. *Tearoom trade: A study of homosexual encounters in public places.* London: Duckworth.

Israel, M., and I. Hay. 2006. *Research ethics for social scientists.* London: Sage.

Johnson, T.S. 2008a. Qualitative research in question: A narrative of disciplinary power with/in the IRB. *Qualitative Inquiry* 14, no. 2: 212–32.

Johnson, T.S. 2008b. *From teacher to lover: Sex scandals in the classroom.* New York: Peter Lang.

Jones, J. 1981. *Bad blood: The Tuskegee syphilis experiment.* New York: Free Press.

Kushner, S. 2006. A lament for the ESRC. *Research Intelligence* 94, February: 9–11.

Lincoln, Y. 2005. Institutional Review Boards and methodological conservatism: The challenge to and from phenomenological paradigms. In *The Sage handbook of qualitative research: Third edition,* ed. N. Denzin and Y. Lincoln, 165–81. Thousand Oaks, CA: Sage.

Macfarlane, B. 2009. *Researching with integrity: The ethics of academic research.* London: Routledge.

Milgram, S. 1974. *Obedience to authority: An experimental view.* New York: Harper & Row.

Mitscherliche, A., and F. Mielke. 1947. *Doctors of infamy: The story of the Nazi medical crimes.* New York: Schuman.

Nind, M., J. Rix, K. Sheehy, and K. Simmons, eds. 2005. *Ethics and research in inclusive education.* London: Routledge/Falmer.

Pieterman, R. 2001. Culture in the risk society: An essay on the rise of a precautionary culture. *Zeitschrift für Rechtssoziologie* 22, no. 2: 145–68.

Piper, H., and I. Stronach. 2008. *Don't touch: The educational story of a panic.* London: Routledge/Falmer.

Power, M. 2004. *The risk management of everything: Rethinking the politics of uncertainty.* London: Demos.

Pring, R. 2000. *Philosophy of educational research.* London: Continuum.

Redfern, M. 2001. *The royal Liverpool children's inquiry report.* London: The Stationery Office.

Redwood, S. 2008. Practitioner enquiry, ethics and the postmodern detective. Paper presented at the Discourse Power Resistance: Cultures in Resistance Conference, March 18–20, in Manchester Metropolitan University.

Richardson, S., and M. McMullan. 2007. Research ethics in the UK: What can sociology learn from health? *Sociology* 41, no. 6: 1115–32.

Scott, C. 2008. Relationships: Ethics committees and research. In *Don't touch: The educational story of a panic,* ed. H. Piper and I. Stronach, chap. 2, 12–22. London: Routledge/Falmer.

Scott, C.L. 2003. Ethics and knowledge in the contemporary university. *Critical Reviews in International Social and Political Philosophy* 6, no. 4: 93–107.

Sikes, P. 2008. At the eye of the storm: An academic(s) experience of moral panic. *Qualitative Inquiry* 14, no. 2: 235–53.

Sikes, P., and H. Piper. 2008. Risky research or researching risk? The real role of ethics review. In *Talking truth confronting power,* ed. J. Satterthwaite, M. Watts, and H. Piper, 51–65. Stoke-on-Trent: Trentham Books.

Sikes, P., and H. Piper. 2010. *Researching sex and lies in the classroom: Allegations of sexual misconduct in schools.* London: Routledge/Falmer.

Simons, H., and R. Usher. 2000. *Situated ethics in educational research.* London: Routledge/Falmer.

Tierney, W., and Z. Blumberg Corwin. 2007. The tensions between academic freedom and Institutional Review Boards. *Qualitative Inquiry* 13, no. 3: 388–98.

Tuhiwai Smith, L. 1999. *Decolonizing methodologies: Research and indigenous peoples.* London: Zed Books.

Pat Sikes and Heather Piper

Socially just research for social justice: negotiating consent and safety in a participatory action research project

Renée DePalma

Facultade de Ciencias da Educación, University of Vigo, Ourense, Spain

This contribution explores what it means to pursue equality and social justice through equitable and just collaborative research methodologies, with a particular focus on two issues: the creation of safe spaces for research participants in the context of a 'dangerous' research topic, and the generation of ethically viable research consent. The data analysed is based on an extended self-study of the ethical issues arising during the *No Outsiders* project, a participatory action research project investigating approaches to lesbian, gay, bisexual and transgender (LGBT) equalities in English primary schools. While we had no particular difficulty securing permissions to conduct the research, our experiences throughout the two and a half year-long project and the debates they generated have suggested that ethical issues emerge within a community as part of the research practice and are better addressed through ongoing discussion than through an external evaluation of potential risk. Further, the insistence on protecting participants through anonymity, while serving an institutional need for litigation protection, can restrict participant agency.

Context: emancipatory action research and *the gay agenda*

Over the course of two and a half years, the *No Outsiders* research team conducted what some might consider to be a 'dangerous' research project: approaches to lesbian, gay, bisexual and transgender (LGBT) equalities in English primary schools. Here I explore what it means to pursue equality and social justice through equitable and just collaborative research methodologies, focusing on a particular research context that came to be defined as controversial (Brettingham 2008a, 2008b) and therefore potentially risky to participants as well as anyone associated with us (colleagues, pupils and even family members). The analysis derives from an extended self-study of the processes and principles operating within the *No Outsiders* project, a UK Economic and Research Council (ESRC) funded project (RES-062-23-0095) that ran from September 2006 to December 2008.[1] The questions defined and explored here emerged in discussion among project team members over the course of the project. Taken together, these discussions critique prevailing notions of informed consent and participant safety and the assumption that a preliminary institutional review process can (or should) define and enforce research ethics.

The *No Outsiders* project involved over 40 participants working in 16 primary education sites and three universities: Sunderland, Exeter, and the Institute of

Education, London. Practitioner researchers worked in primary schools[2] throughout England. University researchers worked closely with practitioner researchers in regional groups, and there were regular individual, regional and national meetings. Some participants kept field notes and journals, and regular individual and small group discussions were later transcribed and used as data. However, much of the data generated by the project took the form of ongoing discussions on an asynchronous, password protected private website, where data could be uploaded for group analysis and discussion, and broader issues relevant to the project could also be debated.

Aside from the traditional action research focus on participants' own practice, university and school-based researchers also made observations about broader school and community contexts that were shared and analysed with the rest of the team and later included in public dissemination in the form of conference presentations, journal articles, books and book chapters. This wider interrogation extended the scope of the research beyond the individual practitioner-researcher and implicated others beyond the research team. The practitioner researchers worked both with colleagues, parents and children in their local practice contexts and with *No Outsiders* team members in the (often virtual) context of the project.

The design of this research called into question many of the binaries that are assumed and reinforced by institutional ethics review boards: Where does practice stop, and research begin? Where do researchers stop, and subjects begin? Where are the boundaries between the school and the research project, when teachers are simultaneously participating as teachers, parents, friends, colleagues and researchers across these boundaries? These questions have featured recently in key debates about how changing understandings of research methodology and, more fundamentally, changing understandings of the nature of knowledge, safety and participation rub up against institutional concerns as manifested in and policed by the aptly titled Institutional Review Board (IRB). Cannella and Lincoln defined the problem as a clash of two different perspectives towards ethics, one 'as a regulatory enterprise, constructing an illusion of the ethical practice of research' and the other as 'particularized understandings and responses that are infused throughout our research practices' (2007, 316–17).

Despite what some might consider the potentially risky and controversial nature of the research (and we have been plagued by tabloid media interest throughout much of the project), we did not have any particular difficulties in securing IRB permissions for the research. Instead, our experience suggests that securing approval did not ensure the ethical nature of our research, nor could it have. The IRB process in its current institutional framework consists of an external evaluation of potential risk, based on the understanding that this risk can and must be eliminated or at least reduced by researchers on behalf of research subjects before the research begins. This may be an admirable goal on some levels, as it is meant to protect subjects from researcher fallibility and even untrustworthiness, but it fails to fully take into account that ethical issues emerge within communities as part of the research practice and need to be negotiated through ongoing discussion. In projects such as ours with a social justice agenda that some might consider risky by nature, whether, when and whom to protect and whether and when to request, provide and withhold consent are complex issues and difficult to separate from the contexts in which they arise.

We understood that our kind of emancipatory action research could very well get us into trouble. We realized early on that issues of consent (determining whose words can be used by whom, and to what purpose) and safety (avoiding risk or litigation) were particularly fraught in research involving primary schools, since children are taken to be particularly vulnerable. Popular prejudices about the particularly sexualized nature of lesbian, gay and bisexual people and essentialized and caricaturized perceptions of trans people cast LGBT people as threatening to children, and any attempt to render these people visible and comprehensible to children has been construed as a form of child abuse in some quarters. While much public response and media coverage was positive (particularly in international contexts), a great deal of sensationalist tabloid coverage expressed a degree of disgust and outrage that constituted association with the project as a risky affair. This risk took various forms for project members, from death threats published on a website to job insecurity to the everyday discomforts involved in justifying the project to wary colleagues and friends. Furthermore, the constant attempts by tabloid media to secure school and participant names constituted risk for colleagues, pupils and even family members. Many of us nervously recalled the scandal that resulted from one headteacher's decision to turn down tickets to a production of *Romeo and Juliet* on the grounds that the play served to propagate heteronormativity; it was this headteacher, rather than the scandal-hungry reporters who stalked her family and camped outside her school gate, who was held accountable in the public eye for the suffering of her colleagues, pupils and family (Philp 1994).

Seeking a socially just methodology: the first advisory group meeting and beyond

As our research was explicitly framed by a social justice agenda, we have been particularly concerned with how the research process itself can be a socially just endeavour. This contribution focuses explicitly on this methodological challenge, not as a means of justifying a claim to recognition as a 'genuinely' just research project, but as a space for exploring the difficult issues which arise when this aspiration is constantly kept in mind. IRB approval, to some extent, became irrelevant to project participants as we began to debate emerging issues of informed consent and participant/subject safety as soon as the project began.

The process of investigating our own concerns and approaches to ethics began when the questions were initially framed and debated during the project's first advisory group meeting, held in October 2006, the second month of the project. All project members were welcome to attend, although teachers' attendance was limited by time constraints, and the external members included representatives from the General Teaching Council for England, the National Union of Teachers, Schools Out, Stonewall[3] and a university-based specialist in sexualities and education. In this first meeting, concerns about safety and informed consent were raised and debated, and a summary of these discussions was posted on the project's web discussion board. These were subsequently debated and discussed in this virtual environment as well as through further advisory group meetings, email exchanges, regional meetings and individual research meetings between university and school-based members. These two main themes (consent and safety) comprised strong threads that continued to focus our discussions along these lines.

Whose consent, and what does it mean to be informed?

The main concerns around consent that arose in our project discussions can be expressed by the following questions:

(1) Whose consent can and should be sought in a collaborative action research project in which teachers' research projects form part of their everyday classroom interventions, yet break new ground in addressing previously silenced subject areas?
(2) In what ways does the controversial nature of the research topic affect the seeking and gaining of consent?

As Guba and Lincoln argue, 'Consent is obtained not only prior to opening the evaluation effort but as information is uncovered and shared; as power relationships shift, this consent must be renegotiated continuously' (1989, 247). This discursive understanding of consent is more in line with a dialogic participatory process (Somekh 2002).

The principle of participation itself, as Homan (2002) points out, is open to deception, where participants are unaware (particularly in the context of participant observation by either 'insider' or 'outsider' researchers) of the extent to which their informal utterances and asides, their body language and their modes of interaction, might be constituted as data and subjected to analysis. And of course, we found that when university researchers or other teachers entered schools, it was impossible to 'turn off' our researchers' gaze. As one university researcher put it:

> My main concern when I was in school on some visits was that people were just not aware what I was doing there and so observing their behaviour/comments and reporting on them seemed very unfair. For example, on my first visit I was in a staffroom where none of the teachers were aware of my role in the school (they were to be told in a meeting later that day), but while I was there they made several comments that I felt were very telling about the nature of the school/attitudes to issues related to the project. At this point, I decided not to take note of their remarks as I felt that I had not been given permission to observe in the school at this point (especially in the staffroom!).

Nevertheless, it was impossible to challenge homophobia in the classroom without taking note of how processes supporting and challenging heteronormativity and heterosexism operated in the broader school contexts. The reluctance of some university researchers to analyse behaviours and comments as data when they took place outside specific classroom practice contexts, as illustrated by this researcher's words, did not prevent some of our classroom teachers from turning the researcher gaze on colleagues. In fact, many teachers described this as unavoidable: participation in the project shaped how they interpreted the world around them, gazing, as it were, through a *No Outsiders* lens that they found impossible to remove.

According to the British Educational Research Association (BERA) Revised Ethical Guidelines for Educational Research, participants include but are not limited to subjects:

> The participants in research may be the active or passive subjects of such processes as observation, inquiry, experiment or test. They may be collaborators or colleagues in the research process or they may simply be part of the context e.g. where students are part of the context but not the subjects of a teacher's research into his or her own professional practice. (1994, 5)

BERA later defines 'voluntary informed consent' as the condition under which all participants, apparently defined as broadly as the above passage suggests, must 'understand and agree to their participation without any duress' (1994, 6). Shortly afterward there is a specific reference to the dilemma of the teacher's dual role of teacher and researcher in action research:

> Researchers engaged in action research must consider the extent to which their own reflective research impinges on others, for example in the case of the dual role of teacher and researcher and the impact on students and colleagues. Dual roles may also introduce explicit tensions in areas such as confidentiality and must be addressed accordingly. (1994, 6)

While this latter observation about action research seems highly insightful and the advice to consider the potential impact is more than reasonable, the juxtaposition of this statement with the extremely broad definition of participants who must provide voluntary informed consent suggests a level of information which might be impractical at best and counterproductive at worst.

In fact, the requirement stipulated by our IRB was that we obtain the written consent of each participating teacher researcher (but not university researchers!) and written permission from the head of each participating school for their school to be involved in the project. Somewhere between BERA's very broad definition of participants who must provide consent (practically everyone) and the rather narrow range of participants whose consent we were actually required to obtain (heads and teacher researchers), there was rather a wide grey area that researchers felt compelled to negotiate throughout the research process.

Homan (2002) among others highlights the potential for deception within received forms of qualitative educational research, where 'informed consent' – for adults and particularly for children – is often given by gatekeepers, such as head teachers and/or class teachers, on behalf of the actual participants of the research. In such situations, the extent to which either gatekeepers or participants know what the research is actually about varies, but it is an accepted tenet of much (including much socially valuable) educational research that to give away too much at the outset would be to influence the findings in an unhelpful way. 'Informed consent' in this situation, and in situations where people have supposedly been given a free choice of participation but are under a number of more or less visible forms of pressure if they don't, becomes assumed consent.

In a sense, we got away with exactly the kind of dodgy gatekeeper consent described above. Particularly given the imminent threat of tabloid journalists waiting outside school gates, we began to consider whether the nature of the research being undertaken in classrooms meant that we needed to go beyond gaining the head's and class teacher's consent, to gaining the consent of children and their parents. There were two problems with this proposition: we began to question the very notion of informed consent, and we began to wonder whether well-meaning attempts to 'inform' might backfire, constructing the project as experimental and dangerous and reinforcing the very homophobic assumptions we were trying to undo. After all, we were trying to provide a space where the silenced could speak and be heard, and we were well aware of the tendency for these marginalized voices to be heard as shouts and unreasonable rants when they first break the silence (DePalma and Atkinson 2009).

Epstein questions the assumption implied by 'informed consent' that research subjects can, at least in some cases, really be informed about the research, 'I realized that if the children lacked a framework for understanding who I was as a researcher, then the notion that they had given their informed consent to the research was, at least, questionable' (1998, 43). This is not meant to imply that children (and parents) are simply not up to the task of comprehending academic research, but that roles are socially defined in school contexts and difficult to modify. In Epstein's case, she found that children had difficulty understanding her position as an adult in the classroom who was not the teacher, since that was the only role that was socially constructed as possible for her adult body. In our case, we found that as difficult as it may be to explain the concept of teacher-researcher to the academic community, this was even more difficult in classrooms, where what the teacher does is teach. Research, if it is conceptualized in educational contexts at all, is not construed as something that might be intertwined with classroom practice. Therefore, simply identifying an everyday educational practice (such as reading a book or drawing a picture) as research imbues it with an air of otherworldliness that did not advance our agenda of inclusion.

In the end, practitioners made their own different choices about whether to take special steps to inform parents and, if so, how to go about that. Of course these decisions were taken after a great deal of discussion with the research group, but teachers took the final decisions. Some consciously refrained from treating their *No Outsiders* work as anything unusual, arguing, for example, that they wouldn't request parent permission or even inform parents upon adopting a new maths curriculum, or if they were going to celebrate Black History Month. Others worried that failure to inform parents before addressing such a 'sensitive' topic in the classroom could stir up an angry response, held parent meetings, sent home announcements in school newsletters, invited parents to attend staff diversity training offered as part of the project, invited parents to preview children's literature associated with the project and/or introduced the project at parent governor meetings. Overall, however, permissions were not requested, as teachers felt that this would further construct LGBT equalities work as something radical, experimental and dangerous.

However, permission was sought for children's images and classroom work to be included in the series of videos that was produced across project schools and in the book written for a professional audience (*No Outsiders* Project Team 2010). This was conceptualized as a different issue altogether, as publication of children's images, particularly in video format where they might be altered and distributed beyond the author's and subject's control, is widely considered to be a threat to children's safety (Child Rights Information Network 2009). This is a broader issue about children, images and predatory virtual spaces and would be impossible to fully explore within the constraints of this contribution, but it is worth mentioning that the 'risky' nature of the research did play a considerable role in these debates. Some argued, for example, that an image of a boy dressed in a feather boa or wearing a bra (over his clothes) in the dress-up corner might be particularly vulnerable if the photo were to fall into the wrong hands, acknowledging the particularly virulent nature of gender-based bullying. Others argued that children who appeared on camera making statements that supported LGBT equalities might be harassed by peers or might reconsider later and regret that their statement had been made public, an argument that would be difficult to make if the child expressed a less controversial and potentially risky opinion. After much discussion of this nature we decided not to make the videos publicly available, as had originally been planned. Project team members were provided with a copy of the videos only after signing an agreement that the videos would only be shown as part of our own presentations and that they would never leave our hands.

In fact, the need to secure written permissions before filming made people nervous that placing such a spotlight on the project might inspire panic. One teacher confided in us that his head teacher was concerned about a potential backlash from parents, who had until then not been worried about the educational practices designed by the teacher as part of the project. This concern was based on the very real danger that parents might withdraw their children from the school, which would have serious financial consequences for an already tightly stretched school budget. Embedded in broader issues about teacher professionalism in an environment of increasingly market-driven curriculum, this situation highlights the concern that parental consent for practiced-based research might paralyse innovation, particularly marginalizing less popular research that fails to market itself successfully.

Safety, and comfort, for all?

The main concerns around safety that arose in our project discussions can be expressed by the following questions:

(1) Who decides whether or not someone needs to be kept safe, who defines this safety, and to what extent are these notions determined by essentialistic and paternalistic notions of safe spaces?
(2) Is it possible to create a space that is safe for all at the same time, or might one person's safety be ignored or even jeopardized in constructing a safe space for another?

The creation of safe spaces is particularly relevant to LGBT equalities work, where minority people are simultaneously unsafe and afforded the possibility of maintaining relative safety, either through invisibility or through the knowledge that they are 'among friends' (DePalma and Atkinson 2009). For pupils, parents and teachers, LGBT equalities work may bring into the open identities and family situations that had been carefully hidden.

This issue came up in the first advisory group meeting as well and, like the questions around negotiating consent, were discussed and debated throughout the project. At the initial advisory group meeting members debated different reactions to a scene in the USA-based documentary *It's elementary: talking about gay issues in school* (Chasnoff 1996), a film that had been shown a couple of weeks before at the first national team meeting. Some members were highly critical of a scene where a child is invited to talk about a contest she entered and won with an essay about her parents, a lesbian couple. As part of her presentation, the child stands before the class and reads the essay aloud. Those who reacted strongly to this episode were not necessarily opposed to the child being open about her parents, but were concerned that this kind of public highlighting of minority children was not an effective or humane social justice strategy. Some pointed to critiques of similar practices in race education, where children were treated as 'examples' of their particular cultural group.

The discussion of this particular case and the broader issues of safety and exposure that it involved was summarized and placed on the website, along with the discussions about consent that were raised at the first advisory group meeting. Later, at a regional meeting where the concern was raised, a teacher said that children are sometimes altogether happy to talk about their LGBT parents, and gave an example from his own school. A university researcher pointed out that children might do things they don't necessarily want to do because they think they should do them, raising issues of power and coercion that can be particularly difficult in classroom situations. Some team members wondered whether by not inviting children to talk about their same-sex relatives and friends, we might actually be adding to the layers of silence and secrecy that construct them as other. Others pointed out that silence and exclusion had become an implicit norm: how could we invite people to speak out without spotlighting them, coercing them, and putting them in danger, even if they seem willing to do so?

As one teacher pointed out, this was something of a no-win situation, as simply reading a story that includes lesbian or gay parents can implicitly spotlight a child if, as often happens, the child's family situation is known but not recognized openly (or, even worse, it has only been recognized in negative terms, in terms of bullying or harassment). Taken to the extreme, schools could become paralysed with fear of implicitly targeting a child; in one school where I interviewed teachers for a previous study, for example, several teachers referred to a particular gender variant child as a reason they might think twice before addressing LGBT issues in the classroom. It is difficult to imagine a way forward in terms of safe practice, let alone safe research, when the mere mention of LGBT people is seen as potentially dangerous to a vulnerable child.

Indeed, the BERA revised ethical guidelines for educational research consider not only risk but also discomfort to be a situation to be avoided in research:

> Researchers must recognize that participants may experience distress or discomfort in the research process and must take all necessary steps to reduce the sense of intrusion and to put them at their ease. They must desist immediately from any actions, ensuing from the research process, that cause emotional or other harm. (1994, 8–9)

The BERA principle of maximizing comfort effectively renders projects like *No Outsiders* impossible, since participation in the project may very well prove to be uncomfortable for LGBT teachers, parents and for children in LGBT-headed families. While some teachers did encourage children to talk about same-sex parents within the broader context of family diversity units and activities, there were no incidents of explicit violence or harassment towards children. However, there may very well have been discomfort, and it is impossible to predict the long-term repercussions on people whose 'controversial' family or personal characteristics are now public knowledge.

In one *No Outsiders* school a lesbian teacher shared information about her own family (and, indirectly, about her own sexuality) as part of a family diversity unit. When a community protest was formed in response to the project in general (focusing mainly on the project books), she felt personally vulnerable and responsible for the vulnerability of her family when the situation developed into an angry conflict. Convinced that her previously positive relationship with the local community had been damaged irreparably, she left her position. Clearly, this was a high-risk situation that, it could be argued, resulted from the introduction of LGBT-themed materials and discussions which included not only this teacher's family diversity unit but a series of lessons involving, among others, books depicting gay, lesbian and non-gender-conforming characters. It was the classroom practice that caused the controversy, but in action research the practice, of course, is integral to the research.

Indeed, one member of a local LGB support group commented to the project director that she should have consulted with the group before conducting such a project in the area, given the high population of LGB people who would be negatively affected by what she considered a predictable response by some segments of the community. The irony here, of course, is that this comment suggests that those very people whose interests we hoped this research would serve might have been likely, if given the chance, to veto the research on the grounds that it could compromise their own safety. It also suggests that the broad interpretation of 'participants' might very well include local minority groups who might be made vulnerable by 'stirring up' controversy, and that even when research team members are willing to assume some degree of risk in the interest of social justice, this risk might leak out into unanticipated sectors.

For participating teachers, taking action to promote LGBT-affirmative school environments may be simultaneously empowering and exposing, whatever the teachers' own sexual orientation. Taking a stand for social justice often requires those who do so to be unsafe, precisely because they are going beyond established norms and paradigms. Given the events described above, it seems clear that it is not only the teacher researcher's safety that needs to be taken into consideration. This consideration does not imply stopping at the first sign of discomfort or concern, but engaging in discussions with local communities can help researchers and others who might be affected become more aware of the operation and circulation of potential risk.

Dialogic vs. institutional risk management

In institutional contexts, however, risk management is not so dialogic. One particular experience has illustrated for *No Outsiders* team members that paternalistic and litigation-driven approaches to risk elimination can interrupt the participant agency involved in efforts like ours to identify and manage risk through internal (and at times, external) negotiations. In the wake of a particularly virulent outbreak of negative tabloid press coverage in September 2008, the university hosting the primary grant-holders exerted pressure to ensure that project members and schools remain anonymous. While anonymity had been maintained voluntarily throughout the first two years of the programme (under recommendation by the ESRC), the team had planned a publicity launch for October 2008 at which teachers were planning to speak openly for the first time about their work on the project. The event was open to the public and media had been invited.

To coincide with the publicity launch, a reporter from the *Times Educational Supplement* (TES) had for the first time been allowed exclusive access to some of the project schools and was planning to release a breaking news article naming schools for the first time. Many of us were nervous about the possible repercussions, but those teachers who had decided to reveal their own and their schools' identities had taken this decision after months of deliberation and discussions within and beyond the project team. As a result of a perceived increase in risk to participants (probably broadly interpreted to include wider school communities), the University of Sunderland upper management, apparently after consultation with ethics, media and public relations teams, 'strongly suggested' to the TES reporter that she not publish schools' and teachers' names, as had been agreed. The publicity launch, which was originally planned to be a press event coinciding with the publication of the TES article, was re-organized as an invitation-only event, closed to the press. Instead of the two articles that had been planned to provide an exclusive insider perspective on the nature of *No Outsiders* work in particular schools, the TES published two articles that implied that project work was stopped by right-wing pressure groups and tabloid media (Brettingham 2008a, 2008b). Many project members, and particularly the teachers who were to be featured in the original version of the articles, were not only upset at being silenced, but angry that the project had been depicted as being forced 'back into the closet' when project work was in fact proceeding as planned in project schools. The TES published a letter from the project director clarifying the situation (Atkinson 2008), but the damage was already done; instead of serving to demystify the project and cast LGBT equalities work in primary schools as just another kind of everyday social justice work, the project was cast as a high-risk endeavour which eventually caved in under pressure from right-wing special interest groups.

Later, at the final project advisory group meeting in late November 2008, this situation was discussed. A teacher who was present, and who had been one of those featured in the originally planned TES article, reiterated that many teachers felt 'extremely saddened' by these events, as instead of finally being given a public forum to describe their work they were silenced. Another member noted that the anonymized articles that the TES published as a result of university pressure to protect participants were in fact quite misleading, and resulted in the widespread belief that the project had been stopped. A researcher based at one of the other two participating universities reported that she recently discovered that a file of incendiary correspondence had been collected and withheld from her for her own (emotional) protection. There was some speculation that the publicity launch lost focus as it shifted from its original plan as a public press event to its later instantiation as an invitation-only press-free event. Everyone understood the university's decision to close down publicity for security reasons, but many project members felt betrayed and silenced by this institutional decision made for their own protection without consultation with them.

It is understandable that a call for death to 'paedo-intellectuals' on a public blog might lead an institution to engage in draconian protective measures. Institutionally, these measures are rooted in the institution's need to protect itself from litigation through predetermined guidelines for doing so effectively. Yet this decision effectively short-circuited the internal negotiation process we as a team had initiated and maintained throughout the project. Many of us were willing to assume some degree of risk and a great deal of discomfort in the interest of pursuing what we had come to perceive as a crucial and under-explored area of social justice. Silence was at the root of the problem we were trying to address, so imposed silence, even for our own protection, undermined our success.

Departing from the premise that education is always an ethical endeavour, Megan Boler argues that while any pedagogy can potentially evoke fear, anger and resistance, sexuality is particularly volatile because of the extent to which it has been relegated to a comfortable silence in classrooms. She calls for a pedagogy of discomfort as a form of collective critical inquiry:

> I outline a pedagogy of discomfort to foreground the question, What do we – educators and students – stand to gain from engaging in the discomforting process of questioning cherished beliefs and assumptions? I begin by defining a pedagogy of discomfort as both an invitation to inquiry as well as a call to action. (1999, 176)

It is important to note that the degree and nature of risks and discomforts endured varied across team members and changed over time throughout the course of experiences and discussions. This suggests that not only is discomfort an implicit aspect of critical inquiry, but that there is no way to determine, in advance, levels of discomfort or even risk that will be universally acceptable. As Boler points out, 'A call to action is not a demand or requirement, but an invitation' (1999, 183).

Beyond institutionally (pre)defined ethics

Throughout the *No Outsiders* project, we have found that maintaining an ongoing debate over key ethics issues that emerged during the course of the project has provided a creative and generative dissensus which has proved far more fruitful than simple consensus over ground rules and procedures. This process has led both to a critique of prevailing notions of participant safety and informed consent and to a consideration of the implications for designing socially just collaborative research in any research context. While the University of Sunderland's IRB required the informed consent of teacher-researchers and their head teachers, we have found that the idealized and well-defined 'participant' implied in this notion of informed consent had little relevance to the complexities of the research process we were engaged in. While our funding institution advocated for participant anonymity and our hosting academic institution eventually imposed such anonymity, we found that many members chafed under such unilateral determinations of acceptable risk levels.

Allen et al. argue for 'a move away from ethics review as a single bureaucratic moment to a continuous, open and critical engagement with ethical issues within a community of researchers' (2009, 139), suggesting that 'a system which offers ethical support might be a more desirable option … in those awkward places, where the most careful and complicated ethical deliberation will be required' (2009, 150). Our experience with an advisory group that took up the task of interrogating ethical issues as they came up and in dialogue with project members supports this recommendation, although it must be admitted that we stumbled upon this idea largely by accident. We had imagined the role of the group more in terms of providing a channel of communication between interested organizations and the research team, but we hadn't imagined ethics considerations to be a significant focus. We were pleasantly surprised when the first meeting set a precedent of thoughtful analysis and lively focused debate. As an alternative (or complement) to the IRB review, we have found our advisory group offered the potential of ongoing critical discussion of issues as they emerged throughout the research process, a much more dynamic and relevant process.

This kind of 'iterative ethics review' process is alluded to in the ESRC's *Research Ethics Framework*:

> RECs (Research Ethics Committees) should have mechanisms that make some provision for future advice and guidance beyond the initial ethics approval process. All research can develop in ways that raise unforeseen ethical implications. This is especially the case in qualitative research where the developing nature of the research agenda, especially over a long period of time, may make it harder to ensure that the rights and dignity of the subject are respected and protected without further review. (2005, 22)

However, while the ESRC envisions this task to be ideally in the hands of university Research Ethics Committees, our experience has suggested that this might turn into paternalistic institutional supervision. Like Allen et al., we envision this review as taking place within a community of researchers, but we have seen a value in also including participants from outside the research group and organizations that have practical, activist, or other agendas that our research might affect. This requires a willingness to listen to and engage with issues across limited understandings and different interests, but we found that this diversity helped to produce meaningful discussions that often went beyond the established wisdom of academia.

In our case, an ethos of serious and critical discussion was established from the very first meeting, and this might have been related to the thoughtfulness and commitment of our particular advisory group members, but it was not automatic even under these circumstances. At the end of the first meeting, which involved rather intense debates, one member asked, 'Is this really what you want us to do?' We actually hadn't planned or even anticipated this role for the advisory group, but we recognized that yes, in fact, that was exactly what we wanted the advisory group to do. This same member also suggested at that point that we might want to refer to the group as an advisory rather than the originally adopted term 'steering group', since steering implies that the locus of control is with the group rather than with the project as a whole. This early shift in terminology actually signalled a second strength of our particular advisory group: the issues raised in advisory group discussions were turned out for the rest of the project team to consider and debate further, rather than as a set of instructions or guidelines to follow.

Cannella and Lincoln critique neoliberal attempts to impose universal research ethics for offering the illusion that concerns about power, morality, and the protection of others can be regulated, arguing that:

> We may or may not ask the philosophical and values questions that would ground ethical constructions of research: Whose knowledge is this? Why (as a researcher) do I choose to construct this problem? What assumptions are hidden within my research practices? How could this work produce exclusions? What do I do as I encounter those unexpected exclusions or oppressions that result from the work? What is my privilege (or power position) in this research? How am I subtly reinscribing my own universals and/or discrediting others? (2007, 316)

In the *No Outsiders* project, we have explored the potential of open discourse as a validity criterion (Heikkinen, Kakkori, and Huttunen 2001) and as an integral part of the research process. Particularly in research projects which seek to employ socially just methodologies by intentionally blurring distinctions between participants and researchers, observers and observed, these kinds of constant self-interrogations need to be built into the research process, independent of and potentially critical of an institutionally defined ethics review process.

Notes

1. With the understanding that they may not necessarily share the interpretations described here, I would like to acknowledge the contribution of the entire *No Outsiders* research team, and particularly that of project director Elizabeth Atkinson.
2. One worked in an early years setting, another worked at local authority level, and another moved from primary teaching into initial teacher training after the first year of the project; the rest were primary teachers, including some headteachers.
3. Schools Out is a UK organization working towards LGBT equality in education (www.schools-out.org.uk) and Stonewall is a UK-based lobbying group supporting LGB rights (www.stonewall.org.uk). Gendered Intelligence, an organization dedicated to understanding gender diversity, was eventually represented at later advisory group meetings (www.genderedintelligence.co.uk).

References

Allen, A., K. Anderson, L. Bristol, Y. Downs, D. O'Neill, N. Watts, and Q. Wu. 2009. Resisting the unethical in formalised ethics: perspectives and experiences. In *Power in the academy*, ed. J. Satterthwaite, H. Piper, and P. Sikes, 135–52. Stoke-on-Trent: Trentham.

Atkinson, E. 2008. *No Outsiders* is alive and well (letter to the editor). *Times Educational Supplement,* October 31. http://www.tes.co.uk//article.aspx?storycode=6004500

Boler, M. 1999. *Feeling power: Emotions and education.* New York: Routledge.

Brettingham, M. 2008a. Gay education in primaries climbs back into the closet. *Times Educational Supplement,* October 17, 20–21.

Brettingham, M. 2008b. Right-wing threats silence gay project. *Times Educational Supplement,* October 17, 1.

British Educational Research Association (BERA). 1994. Revised ethical guidelines for educational research. http://www.bera.ac.uk/blog/category/publications/guidelines/

Cannella, G.S., and Y.S. Lincoln. 2007. Predatory vs. dialogic ethics: Constructing an illusion or ethical practice as the core of research methods. *Qualitative Inquiry* 13, no. 3: 315–35.

Child Rights Information Network. 2009. The use of images of children in the media. http://www.crin.org/resources/infodetail.asp?id=20150 (accessed June 15, 2009)

DePalma, R., and Atkinson, E. 2009. 'Permission to talk about it': LGB and straight teachers' narratives of sexualities equality. *Qualitative Inquiry* 15, no. 7: 876–92.

Economic and Social Research Council (ESRC). 2005. *Research ethics framework.* Swindon: Economic and Social Research Council.

Epstein, D. 1998. Are you a girl or a teacher?: The 'least adult' role in research about gender and sexuality in a primary school. In *Doing research about education,* ed. G. Walford, 27–41. London: Falmer Press.

Guba, E.G., and Y.S. Lincoln. 1989. *Fourth generation evaluation.* Newbury Park, CA: Sage.

Heikkinen, H., L. Kakkori, and R. Huttunen, R. 2001. This is my truth, tell me yours: Some aspects of action research quality in the light of truth theories. *Educational Action Research* 9, no.1: 9–24.

Homan, R. 2002. The principle of assumed consent: the ethics of gatekeeping. In *The ethics of educational research,* ed. M. McNamee and D. Bridges, 23–39. Oxford: Blackwell.

It's elementary: Talking about gay issues in school. Video recording. Chasnoff, D. [Writer] H.S. Cohen and D. Chasnoff [Producer]. USA: New Day Films, 1966.

No Outsiders Project Team. 2010. *Undoing homophobia in primary schools.* Stoke-on-Trent: Trentham.

Philp, R. 1994. Kickoff – controversy over headmistress' refusal to let school children see the Royal Ballet's production of 'Romeo and Juliet' – includes assessment of Dance Magazine awards and the challenge to recognize dancers' accomplishments – Editorial. *Dance Magazine.* http://findarticles.com/p/articles/mi_m1083/is_n4_v68/ai_14986706/

Somekh, B. 2002. Inhabiting each others' castles: Toward knowledge and mutual growth through collaboration. In *Theory and practice in action research: Some international perspectives,* ed. C. Day, J. Elliott, B. Somekh, and R. Winter, 79–104. Oxford: Symposium Books.

One chairperson's experience of ethical review: balancing principle, convention, relationship and risk in educational research

John O'Neill

School of Arts, Development and Health Education, Massey University, Palmerston North, New Zealand

The author's experience of ethical review over six years as an academic member and chairperson of a university human ethics committee has been largely positive and educative. The account brings together archival records and personal experience to create a 'transactive' account of the practical experience of doing ethical review in one university setting. The first part briefly considers the limitations in some common criticisms made of human ethics committees; the second gives a brief personal biography of committee membership; the third uses trend data to exemplify the range of activity in one institutional human ethics committee; and the fourth part uses selected incidents to illustrate discursive tensions of ethical principle, discipline, relationship and risk specific to educational research. The conclusion tentatively suggests some utilitarian steps toward a more informed view of the work of institutional human ethics committees in the review of educational research.

Introduction

When I first read the call for writing about lived experiences of ethics review, I bristled. I feared that a request for stories of personal experience would solicit more polemics 'against the ethicists' (Hammersley 2009, 211) on faceless committees who had supposedly misunderstood, hindered, distorted or otherwise prevented vital, well-designed educational research studies from taking place.

This contribution attempts a corrective to such views by providing a personal narrative of human ethics committee membership (2003–2009) in a university setting that was largely positive and educative. The first part briefly explains my disagreement with some of the more strident criticisms made of human ethics committees. The second gives an institutional and personal backdrop to the discussion. The third provides a discussion of the work of one institutional human ethics committee over a six-year period. The fourth part documents selected incidents and tensions specific to educational research from this period. The conclusion tentatively suggests some utilitarian steps toward a more informed view of the work of institutional human ethics committees.

In New Zealand, institutional ethics committees vary considerably in terms of representation and delegated authority. Some tertiary institutions have a single institution-wide human ethics committee; others a mixture of faculty or discipline committees and a central institutional committee. Generally, committees comprise both academic members and lay or community members. Unusually, as a multi-campus institution, Massey University has three regionally based university-wide committees, overseen by a human ethics chairs committee. Some institutional ethics committees, including Massey University, are accredited by the Health Research Council, which has specific requirements with regard to committee composition, procedures and reporting (see below).

The archival records on which my account is, in large part, based are not in the public domain. The feasibility of the 'study', including its time frame, was initially discussed with the assistant to the vice chancellor (research ethics) who oversees the three regional human ethics committees. Subsequently an application was made to the Massey University Human Ethics Committee (MUHEC) Southern B, and approved (09/40). Permissions were required: to access the Part II (confidential) annual reports of the Human Ethics Chairs Committee (HECC) to Academic Board from the vice chancellor; to access College of Education academic staff from the pro-vice chancellor (education); and to access MUHEC Chairs, past and present, and HECC meeting records from the assistant to the vice chancellor (research ethics). Informed consent to examine individual applications in education and correspondence with the reviewing committee was sought from committee chairs and eligible academic staff in the College of Education via the ethics administrator. Participating academic staff and committee chairs were given the opportunity to comment (factual accuracy and my interpretation) on the draft manuscript.

The account has some limitations which may not immediately be apparent to the reader. Initially, my intention had been to conduct a thematic analysis of the review of all ethics applications in education in the period to identify dilemmas of principle, convention, relationship and risk, and the various ways in which educational researchers and the committee had attempted to resolve these. In the end, a thematic analysis of the entire archive proved overambitious. A significant number of academic staff who may have participated had left the College in the mid-2000s as part of a restructuring exercise. Overall, only 11 of 36 staff completed consent forms. Also, more ethics applications than I had imagined were from multiple staff; some of whom had not given their consent. This reduced even further the pool available for analysis.

Another consideration was the timeline for submission of the initial manuscript – less than eight weeks. Preparation, submission, review and approval of the ethics application for the study took half the available time, leaving one month to gain permissions, recruit participants, retrieve and analyze the archival data. Even though the editors granted me a two-week extension, my writing was rushed, which itself created uncomfortable questions for me, about the completeness of the rendered account.

Finally, lest this account of the processes and people involved in human ethics review at Massey University be read as hagiography, I need to declare my interests. Since submitting the abstract, I applied for and was appointed to the part-time position of director, research ethics, at the University. This has raised some additional personal tensions in meeting the ethical guideline of my scholarly association to report research work 'objectively and frankly, without prejudice' (New Zealand Association for Research in Education 1998, 1.2). So too does the fact that some of the work and interactions I am analyzing are those of close colleagues with whom I have ongoing relationships of trust. Even so, taking account of all these qualifications, I have attempted to ensure the truthfulness of this account in the sense that it does not set out to mislead (Bok 1978, 6) by omission. Similarly, in melding relatively subjective personal experiences with a relatively objective archival record, I have tried to make myself 'immune to procedural criticism' (Blackburn 2005, 30).

The limits of subjective accounts

A simplistic binary opposition is too often drawn between caricatures of all powerful institutional human ethics committees and an all but powerless educational research community. As one who has experience of both, I would argue, instead, that committee members and researchers continuously re-negotiate a complex shared space around the ethics of research in educational settings. Their respective capacities to do so depend on the discourse resources, or material and symbolic capital (Mahar, Harker, and Wilkes 1990, 8) they each have available to them.

To give an extreme (but not implausible) illustration, a renowned, professorial rank education researcher, having won a multi-year, multi-million dollar grant from a prestigious contestable funding pool, applications to which were double-blind reviewed by a panel of international experts, would enjoy a relatively influential position in subsequent interactions with her, or his, institutional human ethics committee. Markers of prestige and status might well remain unstated throughout, but they and their effects would be no less real for all that. The point is that if we are to understand the institutionalized tensions between control and autonomy in educational research ethics, and the manner in which these are realized, we need to identify how power and influence operate in concrete interactions between committees and researchers, rather than assume their distribution in the abstract.

Six years as a committee member (albeit within what may well be an entirely idiosyncratic institutional ethics committee structure) has taught me that the discourse practices (language, behaviour and relations) of ethics committee members and educational researchers both shape and are shaped by the broader cultural discourse of human research ethics. Key strands in this discourse include codified ethical principles, the disciplinary conventions of doing educational research, the relationships that are developed between educational researchers and the social settings in which their research is conducted, and the mitigation of risk of harm to individuals, groups and communities (O'Neill 2008).

These discursive strands manifest relative power, knowledge and voice as committees and researchers attempt to reconcile principles, conventions, relationships and risk in the review of each application. However, in contrast to the apparently widespread view that increasingly bureaucratized institutional ethics committees hold all the power and voice, my experience is that committee members and, especially, committee chairs are acutely aware that their knowledge of the ethics of doing research in particular disciplines, settings and contexts is almost always partial and provisional. They also appreciate that in order to maintain committee credibility, their decisions must secure the broad endorsement of the research communities in which they function. For the most part, discussions take place between the committees and individual researchers or, occasionally, particular research groups, rather than the University academic community as a whole. Nevertheless, these understandings have encouraged a view among the committee chairs of ethical review as, ideally, a supportive, dialogical and educative process. Again, to illustrate the point, at Massey the committees' written decisions on ethics applications are invariably prefaced with the statement:

> Please note that the Committee is always willing to enter into dialogue with applicants over the points made. There may be information that has not been made available to the Committee, or aspects of the research may not have been fully understood.

These seemingly trivial protocols and etiquettes matter. Indeed, following Flyvbjerg (2001), I take the position that in order to understand how the power/knowledge nexus operates in the context of ethical review for committees and educational researchers, it is important to focus on actual practices, before their abstract rules – and to emphasize the little things. Accordingly, this account analyses what is arguably the closest proxy for actual committee practices in this instance: the archive of reports, ethics applications and approval paperwork, related to educational research, accumulated within one institutional ethics committee over a six-year period.

In this sense, I want to do more than simply provide a personal, subjective account, however reflexive (Smyth and Shacklock 1998), of my experience of having been a committee member. I also want to preclude such an account being dismissed as 'armchair non-empirical critique' (Harker, Mahar, and Wilkes 1990, x). Finally, I want to pre-empt accusations that in documenting a positive experience, analysis and theorizing of the experience of ethics committee membership, I might, as Bourdieu has put it, be 'cross[ing] the borders with empty suitcases', that, in effect, I 'have nothing to declare' (Schwibs 1985, in Harker, Mahar, and Wilkes 1990, x).

Constructing a narrative that brings together the archival and the personal in this way, is an attempt to document the qualitative locus of human experience in ethical review, what Eisner refers to as ' transaction, rather than independent subjective and objective entities' (1991, 53). In this regard, readers are left to judge whether my transactive account meets Eisner's tests of trustworthiness: does it ring true, can we agree on its meaning and does it have instrumental utility? (53–60).

Setting the scene

In March 2009, I completed the maximum six-year term as an Academic Board appointee to the local campus committee of the MUHEC. Back in 2002 I had been nominated by my Head of Department, who suggested that I would find the work interesting and challenging, and, moreover, that it would be beneficial to have an academic researcher voice from the College of Education on the human ethics committee. (Since then I have talked informally with other academic appointees to human ethics committees and discovered that most of us shared, to a greater or lesser extent, the same initial personal motivation to educate the committee about the established conventions of research in our disciplines so that our research, and that of colleagues, would not be compromised.)

My first few months on the committee in 2003 were a period of acculturation; learning through participation in the routines and protocols of reviewing applications; working out the subtle idiosyncrasies in the way the chairperson ran our monthly meetings; making personal judgements about the relative strengths, weaknesses, passions and little obsessions of my fellow committee members; identifying potential academic allies; gradually finding the confidence to state and defend personal positions and also to shape discussions around those aspects of ethical review I believed were most important. Initially, I was 'paired' with an experienced committee lay member to prepare summaries of the applications we would present to the committee.

Toward the end of 2003, I was asked to be deputy chair (and, from the end of 2004, chair) of this operational committee, at which point I also became a member of the HECC. This is a sub-committee of Academic Board, the principal academic governance body of the University. The HECC comprises the chairs of the three regional-campus focused MUHECs and, as chairperson, the assistant to the vice chancellor (research ethics), together with the MUHEC secretariat. It meets three times a year. Its role is to oversee the implementation of the Code and ensure consistency of decision-making across the three committees. The HECC prepares annual reports on MUHEC activities for both Academic Board and an external accreditation body, the Health Research Council Ethics Committee.

Accreditation enables the University to review ethics applications from its staff and students that require medical expertise such as invasive procedures, tissue sampling and research with health provider patients, staff or funding, which would otherwise need to be reviewed by a regional Health and Disability Ethics Committee. The Health Research Council's 'Operational Standard' for accredited committees includes criteria for the composition and membership of institutional ethics committees, review and decision procedures, and reporting requirements (Health Research Council 2008). Significantly, in terms of ongoing debates about its applicability to university settings and the social sciences (including education) in particular, the HRC Guidelines claim that 'while the *Operational Standard for Ethics Committees* is written with health research in mind, the principles of ethical review apply to all research' (3). Six of the eight universities in New Zealand have voluntary accreditation status, as do two institutes of technology and one private corporation. MUHEC was first accredited in 1995.

HRC accreditation has undoubtedly contributed to increased and more formalized institutional audit and compliance practices. Equally, in the last 15 years, popular media coverage of two cases of alleged 'Holocaust denial' student research and their investigation at Canterbury and Waikato universities implied inadequate institutional oversight, which has made all universities, including mine, notably more 'risk averse'. Unsurprisingly, the subsequent intensification of ethics oversight by the institution, combined with individual accountability, through the employment agreement, for the 'responsible conduct' of student and staff research (Massey University 2007) has not been universally welcomed by researchers. The trends have been equated, for example, with a lessening of trust in the capacity of researchers to judge how broad ethical principles should be applied in particular circumstances, an obfuscation of the distinction between practical research ethics and abstract bureaucratic control, and an unwillingness by senior staff to question the external imperatives of contract research and the attendant commercialization of universities (e.g. Snook 2003). In criticizing what he sees as harmful bureaucratic creep, Ivan Snook, professor of education, a philosopher and the first chair of MUHEC from 1987 to 1994, pointed out that the committee's initial terms of reference were largely educative and advisory:

(1) to prepare a code of ethics;
(2) to advise and educate staff on ethical matters; and
(3) to ensure that research and teaching involving human subjects conform to the highest ethical standards. (4)

In comparing the 1990 and 2003 versions of the MUHEC Code and application paperwork as evidence of his concerns, Snook's assessment is that 'far from confronting the external realities and subjecting them to critical scrutiny, ethics committees have become more inward looking and bureaucratic' (Snook 2003, 11).

My experience of committee membership would lead me to disagree with this assessment, noting, for instance, that the contemporary context for staff and student research in education differs markedly from that in 1987 when the MUHEC committee was first established. Most notably, in my view, there has been a considerable increase in the amount of educational research undertaken by a much larger body of students and staff seeking postgraduate credentials in a merged teachers' college and university faculty (see Scott and Fonesca 2010); similarly, the proportions of this research undertaken by relatively inexperienced researchers, both staff and students, have grown in education as they have across the social sciences. In contrast, the time available for collegial discussion of and informal learning about the ethics of educational research has diminished, while timelines for the completion of research, both disinterested and contract, have tightened. Finally, the sheer volume of applications reviewed by an institutional ethics committee means that it is no longer possible to meet with all applicants. In most cases, the application paperwork therefore has to serve also as an ersatz form of face-to-face discussion, the norm when MUHEC was first established. All of these trends help explain the need for and growth in institutional checks and balances in the domain of educational research ethics – to label all of this 'increased bureaucracy' is to overlook the practical consequences of the 'massification' and 'credential inflation' that have occurred in postgraduate study in recent years.

Unpalatable as it may be, to understand the logic behind increased surveillance of research ethics in our discipline, and even allowing for the fact that much of it is postgraduate research 'training', we should also probably be honest enough to concede that at least some educational research proposals reviewed by institutional ethics committees are quite simply inadequate. As Snook rightly comments, 'badly conducted research can have important ethical implications' (2003, 8). However, this too fails to articulate the possibility that badly conducted research may also be badly designed research. In my experience, ethics committees fulfil an important role in ensuring that poorly conceived educational research is challenged on ethical grounds. While committees do struggle, on occasions, to distinguish between 'unethical' and 'inadequate' research, and although there may also be considerable disagreements among committee members on matters of epistemology, ontology or axiology, the key point is that committee discussion typically focuses on the adequacy of the justification provided by the researcher, rather than *a priori* assumptions by the committee about how a particular study should be designed and conducted.

The archival record

This part of the narrative presents trend data compiled from annual reports of the HECC to Academic Board and HRCEC, 2003–2008. (Some but not all education research is reported separately in these documents.) The aim here is to report relevant education data in the context of overall University ethical review of human participant research for the period when I was a committee member.

Consistent with the original educative, collegial approach to the establishment of its code of ethics, Massey University operates a 'high trust' model in which staff are delegated the responsibility to undertake peer review assessments of the ethics of proposed research. Equally, unlike HDECs, there is no ongoing monitoring and review of the ethics of approved research studies. It is left to applicants to return to the committee if ethical issues arise, or if amendments are necessary to the approved protocol. A screening questionnaire is used in conjunction with the MUHEC Code to determine whether a full application is required to be submitted for whole committee review. The questionnaire is intended to help researchers decide, first, whether the potential harm of the study is greater than that normally encountered in everyday life; and, second, whether there are particular ethical issues related to each of the principles of the Code, that merit committee review. If not, the researcher may choose to submit a notification of the study to the Research Ethics Office, where it is recorded on a database and included in the summary report to Academic Board each year. Increasingly, scholarly journals and some research grant awarding bodies require evidence of committee approval, and this is reflected in the gradually increasing numbers of 'low risk' applications.

Over the past six years the proportion of committee reviewed applications has fallen from approximately two-thirds to one-third of the total. Education research, a fifth of all recorded University research in 2003, has declined by nearly half in the last three years, possibly as a direct result of reductions in staff and postgraduate student numbers in the College compared with the wider University, and the introduction of 'coursework only' study pathways at masters level.

The MUHEC Code covers research, teaching and evaluations of University services. Among full applications to committees, on average a third were from staff over the six years, and nearly two-thirds from students. Assuming an even distribution of education applications across the three operational committees, the number reviewed by each would have declined from 20 per annum to 10 per annum in 2008, or about one per committee each month.

An average of a fifth of 'low risk' notifications was for staff research and three-quarters were student research. Education notifications follow a similar pattern to notifications across the University, declining from a fifth to nearly half that proportion by 2008.

Each MUHEC operational committee has up to six community or lay members, up to four academic members, and up to two Vice Chancellor nominees (a category used to fill gaps in the expertise categories required for HRCEC accreditation such as ethical, legal, medical practitioner or cultural expertise). Table 1 summarizes the educational expertise among academic and community committee members across the three operational committees. Expertise was defined as one or more of a degree in education, a professional teaching qualification, or research experience in education. Although numbers have declined overall, each committee had a minimum of two members with educational expertise each year.

The HRCEC Operational Standard also specifies four categories of decision on applications: unconditionally approved, provisionally approved, deferred, declined. Provisional approval covers everything from minor typographical corrections and the insertion of standard committee statements, to requests for major revisions; applications are deferred when the committee judges that it has insufficient information to review the application. On average, about one-eighth of applications each year were deferred or declined, the majority of these deferred (Table 2). The great majority of applications each year were provisionally approved. For this category of decision, the committee chairperson has delegated authority to approve applicant responses to

Table 1. Committee members with education expertise.

	All	
	N	Ed
2003	36	13
2004	29	13
2005	34	12
2006	32	9
2007	35	9
2008	34	8

Table 2. Committee decisions.

	N	Approve	Provisional	Defer	Decline	Other
2003	290	33	208	38	4	7
2004	322	69	225	27	1	0
2005	290	26	229	32	2	1
2006	223	19	181	19	1	3
2007	210	17	158	32	0	3
2008	220	21	168	29	2	0

queries or request for revisions that are sent to each applicant as minutes within 10 days of each monthly meeting. Authority is delegated on the premise that all necessary ethical issues in the proposed research have been canvassed to the satisfaction of the committee.

Anecdotal evidence from some academics would suggest that institutional ethics committees frequently delay research. Committee approval statistics suggest that delays occur only in a small proportion of applications, and these for reasons which may be beyond the control of the committee. At Massey University, each of the three operational committees meets monthly for 11 months each year. Applicants are required to submit applications two weeks beforehand and are guaranteed a decision within 10 days of the committee meeting. Staff and students are advised to allow six to eight weeks for ethics approval in their research designs. There is also a provision, rarely requested, for the 'expedited review' of applications where, for example, the deadlines of external commissioning or funding bodies require urgency. Table 3 summarizes the delays, in months, for applications made by staff and students in education. Some deferred applications were approved within the routine eight weeks. Most of the 'no outcome' figures occur because the outcomes were finalized following the annual report to Academic Board, which is prepared mid-year. (A separate check on outstanding decisions by the ethics administrators revealed that three of these were recorded as withdrawn and 10 approved. In a further five cases, applicants had not responded to committee correspondence or periodic administrator follow-up.)

Incidents and tensions

In this section, four incidents illustrate the tensile interactions that routinely occur between committees and researchers. Each of the four incidents is linked to one of the

Table 3. Education applications with deferred or delayed outcomes.

		Delay		Months to outcome				No outcome	
	N	Student	Staff	0–2	2–3	3–4	4–5+	Student	Staff
2003	58	12	5	2	3	2	4	1	5
2004	66	9	4	2	3	2	2	3	1
2005	62	17	8	3	7	6	6	2	1
2006	34	9	4	3	3	2	3	2	0
2007	38	9	4	1	5	1	2	2	2
2008	30	5	3	2	3	1	1	1	0

discursive strands above (principle, discipline, relationship and risk) but the discussion focuses on tensions between them. My experience is that these tensions are precisely what institutional ethics committees are required to consider, and reconcile, in order to make decisions about particular applications. Moreover, as is shown across the range of examples, power, knowledge and voice are exercised diversely and not uniquely vested in operational ethics committees that review applications from researchers.

Principle

One of the eight ethical principles in the MUHEC Code is 'minimisation of harm to participants, researchers, institutions and groups' (Massey University 2006, 4). The Code also makes the point that, unlike rules, principles 'are very general and need to be interpreted before being applied in a context' (4). Commonly, students and staff in education wish to undertake small-scale research involving colleagues or students in their own institution in order to understand and influence practice for the better. In one application (09/40 Doc 13) a researcher wanted to investigate colleagues' experiences of major organizational change in a tertiary education institution.

The minutes note that the application was deferred because the committee 'believed there were significant issues in the application' relating to access of potential participants, some of whom were no longer employed at the institution, the guarantees of anonymity that were proposed by the researcher and the fact that eligible participants might be identifiable if they were accessed via a line manager, as proposed. The committee wished to see 'a broader consideration of potential risk to participants and [had] concerns regarding confidentiality of the proposed data collection method'. The application was withdrawn by the researcher and a new application submitted a few weeks later (09/40 Doc 17). This was provisionally approved by the committee subject to clarification of participant recruitment and possible harm through identification (the proposed sample was small), clarity on the likelihood that the tertiary institution would be identified in publications (through the author affiliation) and the provision of counselling information (should any participant still be experiencing discomfort as a result of the organizational change).

In this case, the researcher's interpretation and application of the principle of minimizing harm was based on personal experience of the organizational change being investigated. This, it was suggested, gave the researcher the capacity to understand the personal and interpersonal issues that would likely emerge from the data, to empathize with participants and therefore to identify and mitigate any potential harm to participants. In contrast, the committee's position was that a broader analysis of potential harm to participants was needed because some participants' personal experiences might be quite different to the researcher's own. The committee's position was not that the proposed research was inherently likely to cause harm, and therefore should not proceed, but simply that a more detailed consideration needed to be given to the identification and mitigation of possible harm to individuals and the institution.

I recall that a focus of committee discussion was that research on contested organizational change in education was, in principle, very worthwhile. In part, this was precisely because such change may well be experienced very negatively by some individuals, and that in extreme cases such experience may either be ongoing, or resurface through participation in the study (a particular concern of the medical practitioners on the committee). To exclude such participants from the research on the grounds of avoiding harm altogether might reasonably have been challenged using another of the eight ethical principles in the Code, namely 'justice'. In this instance, the committee suggested the provision of counselling information as adequate recognition that the participation could cause distress to some participants, and in fulfilment of the researcher's obligation to provide for this possibility.

While the example may appear banal or trivial, it is important to note the deliberate positioning of the reviewing committee with regard to the proposed research. In deciding to defer the first application, the committee determined only that it had received insufficient information from the applicant to assess the ethics of the proposed research against several key ethical principles including potential harm, and the rights of participants to confidentiality and fully informed consent. In the revised application, these same issues of clarification were explored a little further with the applicant to the point where the committee was satisfied that the ethical principles were being understood and applied. Throughout its correspondence with the researcher, the committee offered a rationale for each of its queries, linked explicitly to the principles in the Code.

Routinely, discussions in the HECC reiterate the need to ensure committee discussions and correspondence with applicants are always framed in terms of the ethical principles contained in the MUHEC Code. In my experience, the operational committees review numerous applications to conduct 'insider' educational research and have, over time, developed collective skills in the identification, avoidance and mitigation of potential harm, so that research may proceed more smoothly. No doubt this understanding has been helped by having several members on the committee, academic and lay, with education expertise. Nevertheless, the key assertion I wish to make is that the committee may often have greater collective understanding than the researcher of the 'fishhooks and broken glass' that are latent in the practical application of abstract ethical principles to seemingly straightforward, familiar research contexts.

Discipline

I noted above a trend toward increased 'risk management' of research ethics by the central University since the identification of alleged shortcomings in the supervision of student research at other universities nationally. One of the casualties of greater central monitoring and control of human ethics review at Massey University has been the diminution in status of the College of Education ethics committee from one that exercised autonomy in judging whether to approve ethics applications from staff and students, or to require that they be submitted for review by MUHEC, to one which could provide informal peer review only within a more tightly administered ethics notification-application system. (This occurred sometime before I joined MUHEC in 2003.) One of the perceived advantages of ethical review of research undertaken by colleagues in education was the claim that they would 'understand' educational research better than researchers in other disciplines in the social sciences, or from other colleges within the University.

References to educational research issues regularly appeared in the minutes of the HECC between 2003 and 2008 (09/40 Docs 019–025). The issues were both procedural (a request from the College for a template for seeking organizational consent) and substantive (whether the Code should refer to competency rather than age of assent/consent for children to participate in research). The extract which follows is from a memorandum from the HECC chairperson to the pro vice chancellor (education):

> *Guidelines for use of videos filmed during a research project*
>
> Recently MUHEC: PN considered an application for ethics approval for a project which involved videoing children. The researchers proposed that the videos would be used for teaching purposes and conference presentations after the project had finished. MUHEC: PN considers that it would be helpful if the College of Education prepared guidelines concerning the use of such videos. Issues that might be considered include:
>
> - Period for which videos would be held for teaching and/or conference use.
> - Permission of parents/caregivers for all uses that might occur after the research is completed.
> - Context in which clips might be presented, i.e. positive or negative.
> - Publication of clips on a website.
>
> If guidelines are developed, I would be grateful for a copy. They could then be incorporated into the human ethics website for others who might be seeking guidance. Guidelines would then also assist MUHEC in assessing future applications from the College of Education. (09/40 Doc 20)

In practice the memorandum simply formalized a discussion that had taken place in the HECC. The chairperson of the College peer review committee was invited to provide advice and then consult with two operational committee chairs (with legal and research expertise on the use of images) on the parameters of the guidelines. The incident illustrates one attempt by the HECC to draw on particular disciplinary expertise in education to develop guidelines relevant to staff across the University. More broadly, it also signals a disposition toward the incorporation of disciplinary expertise in the development of shared practical guidelines to interpret abstract ethical principles for use by researchers and committee members.

Relationship

Over the six-year period, 2003–2008, a total of seven formal complaints were made. Three concerned committee decisions, two about ownership of research data, one unspecified and one about the performance of a committee. Correspondence between researchers and the operational committee chairs occurs more frequently. Among the HECC minutes, there was one incident reported to the chairs committee that was specific to the issue of conducting research in educational settings and the role of the human ethics committee in deciding whether research had sufficient educational merit to proceed (09/40 Doc 25). This issue relates directly to two statements in the Code. One of these refers to research involving children and derives from a basic principle in medical research ethics:

> Research requiring children as participants should not be undertaken unless there is a specific and demonstrable need to perform the research on children and no other reasonable route to the relevant knowledge is available. (Massey University 2006, 15)

The other concerns the ethical principle of distributive justice, its practical interpretation in terms of the 'fair distribution of the benefits and burdens of research within a particular population' (Massey University 2006, 13) and, specifically, the commonplace practice of 'convenience sampling' of children for research through institutions such as schools. In this respect, the Code states that 'research participants should not be selected simply because they are readily available in settings where research is conducted' (13). While this frames the tension specifically in terms of an ethical principle, a larger issue has to do with the nature of the relationships established between researchers and the communities in which they conduct their investigations, including schools.

Where these relationships are longer term, and where direct benefits accrue to the students and teachers, suggestions of convenience sampling by researchers are less likely to be raised. Comparatively few educational research proposals reviewed during my six years on the committee were explicitly based on the aim of mutually beneficial relations between researchers and participants; where this was the case it was usually research involving early childhood education researchers or studies that had adopted kaupapa Māori (indigenous) emancipatory research approaches, where the study focus itself was negotiated with local communities.

One of the 'tests' applied by the operational committees in assessing the proposal to access children in schools is 'immediate educational relevance' or whether the proposed study is likely to be directly beneficial to the students and children in the setting. Another is whether the sample could readily be identified and recruited from outside the educational setting. Both these questions are often raised by those with education expertise on the committees.

In this particular incident, a senior researcher had raised several issues about decision-making in correspondence with the chair of the operational committee, including the role it appeared to exercise in approving (or withholding) access to schools to researchers:

> It is, in my opinion, entirely inappropriate for a Massey committee to be assuming the role of protecting/preventing the public schools from having links with academic research. The themes of the current project [are] an issue of considerable interest to schools, to teachers and to parents … Principals, teachers, parents and the children themselves are all given the opportunity to agree to spend some time as participants in the research … It should not be up to MUHEC to attempt to control this process … especially since the concept of 'immediate educational significance' will be hard to define. As I responded to the committee at our meeting, of course schools are a convenient, i.e. appropriate, way to contact families and access children in a safe and comfortable environment, however the tone of this word implies some sort of underhand or lazy way of carrying out research, and I resent the implication. (09/40 Doc 26)

In their discussions of the correspondence, the chairs noted (09/40 Doc 25) that the committees were aware that often schools approached to participate might simply take committee approval as evidence of the educational benefits of the research and not question further. Equally, experience suggested that applications to the committees from teachers or principals themselves (as postgraduate students) could often lack knowledge of ethics processes. In the suggestions for a written reply from the chairperson of the HECC to the researcher, were that committees needed to adhere to the Code (including the principle of justice) in making their decisions, but that the role of the committee as 'gatekeepers' to research in educational settings would be included as a topic at the next professional development workshop for MUHEC committee members. It was also noted for the reply that the Operational Standard for accredited committees contained similar ethical principles regarding the use of specific populations for studies and that the University should be adhering to the highest possible ethical standards.

In this instance, the claim of 'gatekeeping' was framed in terms of the research relationship between researchers and schools. More generally, the composition of institutional ethics committees, with both academic and lay members, makes possible the articulation of questions regarding the 'good' or 'benefit' of a proposed study that may not naturally arise within faculty or discipline-based review processes. My experience has been that lay or community members often ask quite pointed questions about the claimed relevance of a study to a particular community or population sample, while academic members from other disciplines frequently challenge the claimed knowledge benefits that will accrue. Indeed, in the absence of longer term relationships between researchers and educational settings, it might reasonably be argued that an important ethical role of an institutional ethics committee is to pose precisely these sorts of questions on behalf of potential participants and their communities.

Risk

One of the roles of MUHEC is to protect the rights of both researchers and participants, and to attempt to balance these in the application of the ethical principles that constitute the Code. In 2003, many applications (both staff and student) were presented to the operational committee I sat on, including several in education, which relied on semi-structured interviews with relatively small numbers of informants for data gathering. Comparatively few of these either provided explicitly for informant checking of transcripts, or adequately explained the theoretical or methodological framework that would be adopted for data analysis, despite the potential sensitivity of some of the proposed topics. The committee observed that little consideration appeared to be given by applicants to the possibility that misunderstandings might occur over what was disclosed by participants, its meaning, and whether, on reflection, participants would want everything they had said to be included. (I recall mentioning my own experience of conducting an elite interview with a senior educationist in government who was quite happy to talk openly during the interview, but subsequently deleted most of the transcript including all of the interesting sections.)

This prompted discussion on the potential benefits to participants and researchers of addressing interview transcripts in the Code, in terms of the principle of fully informed consent: participants would routinely have an opportunity to edit their interview transcript after the event, while researchers would have a record of approval from the researcher to use the edited transcript for research. The committee discussed alternatives, for example that some researchers might wish to preserve the authenticity of the interview discourse, and others might wish to offer participants the opportunity to comment on the analysis of interview data. In the end, the verification of transcripts was seen as a workable norm in terms of balancing rights and responsibilities and any 'risk' associated with a breach of these in most applications. I offered to draft wording and an associated template for use by researchers.

Taking into account the substance of the committee discussion, the Code was reworded to state that 'normally, transcripts of interviews should be provided to participants for editing. If the researcher considers that the right of the participants to edit is inappropriate, a justification would need to be made to the committee' (09/40 Doc 19). At a subsequent HECC committee meeting, one chair objected strongly to this change on the grounds that it failed to acknowledge that 'most of the individual-interview-based research that we do is conducted from a social constructionist epistemological framework'. Thus, the requirement made no sense for many researchers in the social sciences, including education, particularly for anyone using 'methodologies of discourse analysis, narrative analysis, conversation analysis and several other methodologies'. Moreover, it was argued that requiring researchers 'to justify this stance to the committee appears to merely privilege research making positivist assumptions and ignore the fact that valid research may be conducted from other, quite different, assumptions'. The chair's analysis then broadened to the relationship between committees and researchers generally, and the need for MUHEC to exercise caution in acting in ways that might be seen to circumscribe the conception and conduct of research:

> In seeking to make the application process smoother for applicants, this particular form appears to me to be unnecessary and yet another hurdle to put in front of researchers doing constructionist research merely because the [ethics committees] do not appear to understand the nature of this research. It would seem to me that if the committee does not understand why a particular project is proceeding in a particular way, they can request justification from the researcher and learn from the experience. The committee should not institutionalise procedures aimed against specific forms of data collection, and should always recognise that every project needs to have its ethical issues evaluated within the context of the specific procedures of that project. (09/40 Doc 019)

In this case, the procedural error was in not fully debating the proposed change on HECC prior to implementation. The point of the incident, though, is to illustrate the regular discussions among committee chairs of the need to strive for a workable balance between academic freedoms and responsibilities in the application of the principles of human research ethics.

Conclusion

Stories are always recounted by their teller to convey particular messages. In constructing my 'story' from quantitative and qualitative data, and subjective and objective sources, it is to be hoped that a rich account about the discursive nature of human ethics committee membership and work has emerged, one that at least rings true. From this transactive account, I would hope also that certain practical imperatives for promoting dialogical, collegial relations between education researchers and institutional ethics committees suggest themselves. First, education researchers and committee members might usefully conceptualize their interactions not as compliance but as conversations around the interpretation and application of shared ethical principles. Second, my experience would suggest that institution-wide ethics committees need to comprise both academic and community members with a range of knowledge and skills; but that in order to review education research applications they also need to have, or co-opt, members with research experience in the discipline of education. Third, education researchers must have opportunities to educate committee members about the practical ethical issues and tensions they face in the conduct of their research, particularly following ethical approval. And, finally, education researchers must, for their part, accept collective responsibility to address the ethical and methodological shortcomings that feature, more than occasionally, in research applications reviewed by institutional ethics committees.

References

Blackburn, S. 2005. *Truth: A guide for the perplexed.* London: Allen Lane.

Bok, S. 1978. *Lying: Moral choice in public and private life.* Hassocks, Sussex: Harvester Press.

Eisner, E. 1991. *The enlightened eye: Qualitative inquiry and the enhancement of educational practice.* New York: Macmillan.

Flyvbjerg, B. 2001. *Making social science matter: Why social inquiry fails and how it can succeed again.* Cambridge: Cambridge University Press.

Hammersley, M. 2009. Against the ethicists: On the evils of ethical regulation. *International Journal of Social Research Methodology* 12, no. 3: 211–25.

Harker, R., C. Mahar, and C. Wilkes. 1990. Editors' introduction. In *An introduction to the work of Pierre Bourdieu: The practice of theory,* ed. R. Harker, C. Mahar, and C. Wilkes, ix–xiv. Houndmills, UK: Macmillan.

Health Research Council. 2008. *HRC guidelines for ethics committee accreditation.* http://www.hrc.govt.nz/root/Ethics/Ethics%20Overview/Accredited_Ethics_Committees.html (accessed August 31, 2009).

Mahar, C., R. Harker, and C. Wilkes. 1990. The basic theoretical position. In *An introduction to the work of Pierre Bourdieu: The practice of theory,* ed. R. Harker, C. Mahar, and C. Wilkes, 3–25. Houndmills, UK: Macmillan.

Massey University. 2006. *Code of ethical conduct for research, teaching and evaluations involving human participants.* http://www.massey.ac.nz/massey/research/ethics/human-ethics/code/code.cfm (accessed August 31, 2009).

Massey University. 2007. *Code of responsible research conduct and procedures for dealing with misconduct in research.* http://policyguide.massey.ac.nz/ (accessed August 31, 2009).

New Zealand Association for Research in Education. 1998. *Ethical guidelines.* http://www.nzare.org.nz (accessed August 31, 2009).

O'Neill, J. 2008. Safe ethics for researching teachers' work. *New Zealand Journal of Educational Studies* 43, no. 1: 51–64.

Schwibs, B. 1985. 'Bernd Schwibs gespräch mit Pierre Bourdieu' [Bernd Schwibs in conversation with Pierre Bourdieu]. *Neu Sammlung* 3. Stuttgart: Klett-Cotta.

Scott, C., and L. Fonseca. 2010. Overstepping the mark: Ethics procedures, risky research and education researchers. *International Journal of Research & Method in Education* 33, no. 3: 287–300.

Smyth, J., and G. Shacklock. 1998. Behind the 'cleansing' of socially critical research accounts. In *Being reflexive in critical educational and social research,* ed. G. Shacklock and J. Smyth, 1–12. London: Falmer.

Snook, I. 2003. Are ethics committees ethical? Paper presented to the annual conference of the New Zealand Association for Research in Education, December, in Christchurch.

Research ethics and participatory research in an interdisciplinary technology-enhanced learning project

Frances Tracy and Patrick Carmichael

Faculty of Education, Community and Leisure, Liverpool John Moores University, Liverpool, UK

This account identifies some of the tensions that became apparent in a large interdisciplinary technology-enhanced learning project as its members attempted to maintain their commitment to responsive, participatory research and development in naturalistic research settings while also 'enacting' these commitments in formal research review processes. It discusses how these review processes were accompanied by a commitment to continuing discussion and elaboration across an extended research team and to a view of ethical practice as an aspect of *phronesis* or 'practical wisdom' which demands understanding of specific situations and reference to prior experience. In this respect the interdisciplinary nature of the project allows the diverse experience of the project team to be brought into play, with ethical issues a joint point of focus for continuing interdisciplinary discourse.

Introduction

This account discusses challenges faced by a major interdisciplinary technology-enhanced learning project as it has developed an ethical framework to inform its research activities and patterns of engagement with a range of participants in different settings and with different disciplinary practices. The 'Ensemble: Semantic Technologies for the Enhancement of Case Based Learning' project runs for three years from October 2008 to 2011, one of eight projects under the joint Economic and Social Research Council (ESRC) and Engineering and Physical Sciences Research Council (EPSRC) Technology Enhanced Learning Phase of the Teaching and Learning Research Programme (Pollard 2007). The project is exploring the potential of technologies associated with the emerging 'semantic web' (Berners-Lee, Hendler, and Lassila 2001; Shadbolt, Berners-Lee, and Hall 2006) to support teaching in complex, controversial and rapidly evolving fields where case-based learning is the chosen pedagogical approach. The semantic web is envisaged as a 'web of data' in which heterogeneous resources (qualitative and quantitative, images, audio, video and text) are available for users (in this case, teachers and students in higher education) to engage with them in creative and generative ways. It represents a major programme of technological development, with new pedagogical opportunities and challenges.

The research involves the participation of teachers and undergraduate and post-graduate students in two distinctive higher education institutions. It seeks to explore the nature and role of the cases around which learning is focused, and the contribution of emerging technologies and techniques in supporting this learning. The project has features which presented particular challenges for research design, methodologies and ethical practice, including:

- Diversity in settings and research perspectives: while all the project research settings use some kinds of 'cases' in teaching and learning, these have different roles, structure and scope. The pedagogical practices and discourses that accompany them are widely varied (Tscholl, Tracy, and Carmichael 2009) and the research team themselves have brought differing experiences and commitments, enacted through varied research practices. Rimpilainen and Edwards (2009) discuss how different 'hinterlands' were enacted in a single research setting.
- The use of technology in the research process: the project has used a range of technologies and techniques to collect data and support interpretation and analysis. These 'technology-enhanced research' approaches offer potential to gather new forms of data (e.g. logs of online activity), to amass large volumes of data collected over long periods and to carry out primary and secondary analysis for which provision of fully 'informed consent' might be impossible.
- Commitments to participatory design and research: there is a commitment to involve participants not just as respondents or in the generation of 'user requirements' but also in recruiting other participants, research design, design and evaluation of technological tools, co-interpretation of data, and in the dissemination and sustainability of the project. This has offered not only opportunities for participants to inform and shape the project but also places upon them new responsibilities, particularly involvement in innovations that could change the experience of other teachers or learners.
- Directed but unpredictable changes in pedagogical practice and technologies: given the participatory nature of the project, while not conceived as a programme of technological 'interventions', part of the work of the project is the development of new technological tools to be introduced into teaching and learning. These will change practices, discourses and relationships and have impacts on learning outcomes. The extended engagement of participants with the project also had the potential to frame their reflections on existing practice, inform innovations and change relationships within and beyond classroom settings.

We return to these themes in relation to ethical review and research practices in different settings.

The project as an interdisciplinary community of inquiry

The diversity of the research settings is matched by the diversity of the Ensemble project team, which includes researchers with backgrounds in computer sciences, information science, cognitive sciences, social sciences and education; specialists in teaching and learning in specific disciplinary settings; two PhD students conducting their own projects; and contributing student researchers through an Undergraduate

Research Opportunities Scheme. Many of the team have worked in multiple disciplinary or professional settings. While some characterize themselves as 'discipline-hoppers' or 'boundary-crossers' (echoing Wenger's (1998) notion of 'brokers' as belonging to multiple communities of practice, able to participate in the meaning-making practices of each), what is evident is a variety of what Hall (1999) calls 'personal pan-disciplinarity', common in emerging fields such as technology-enhanced learning.

Working across disciplines has often been understood to involve bringing together teams of individuals with diverse expertise, to solve comparatively well-defined (or *predefined*) problems. An educational software development project might include educational researchers, systems analysts, programmers, user interface designers and so on. A distinction is sometimes drawn between *multidisciplinary* activity and *interdisciplinary* research (Austin, Park, and Goble 2008, 559). While multidisciplinary working involves several disciplines contributing knowledge and methods to solve problems or provide generalized interpretations (Dogan and Pahre 1990; Austin, Park, and Goble 2008), interdisciplinary work goes further and leads to integrative understanding (Kokelmanns 1979). Barry, Born, and Weszkalnys (2008) highlight alternative contemporary approaches to interdisciplinarity and interdisciplinary working which challenge the 'autonomy' of disciplines, particularly in the sciences (Nowotny, Scott, and Gibbons 2001). One outcome of this model of interdisciplinary working may be participants' reflection on their existing disciplinary practices, leading to new conceptualizations of accountability and quality (Strathern 2004).

These approaches fit within what Hakkarainen et al. (2004, 11) describe as the 'knowledge creation' metaphor for learning, involving the deliberate advancement of knowledge, tools and associated social practices and discourses. Knowledge creation builds on existing cultural and community knowledge, exposed through structured enquiries (Haythornthwaite 2006) and genres of 'conversation' (Patel and Solomon 2009).

A further exploration of interdisciplinary working by Hall (1999) describes 'cultures of inquiry' as complex and contested domains in which participants have been differently 'disciplined', have diverse standpoints and commitments, and which can support the discursive construction of multiple narratives, enriched and advanced through formative critique. He extends this model to social enquiry more generally, mapping the 'generalizing' and 'particularizing' practices employed by researchers which can contribute to collective understandings and the creation of new approaches.

The Ensemble team's response to the interdisciplinary complexity of the project has been twofold. First, there has been a conceptualization of the project as a culture of inquiry, characterized by 'conversations' and processes of collaborative interpretation. Second, these conversations (through face-to-face discussions, team working, collaborative writing, and the sharing of readings, resources and examples) have been directed to a series of points of focus (Wenger), specificities (Haythornthwaite) or generalizing and particularizing practices (Hall). Two areas that promote the most engaging discussions across the entire team are those of *participation* and *ethical frameworks*, both complex and contested in their own right, with discourses around them that raise 'creative tensions'. The Project's expansive idea of participation presented dilemmas and challenges in relation to ethical frameworks and the specifics of ethical review.

The participatory practices of the project

The commitment of the project to be 'participatory' led to wide-ranging discussions; the project's understanding of participation has been a broad one. Like Elliot (2006) and Boser (2006) we see participatory research as involving engagement at all stages and in all key deliberations. Team discussions drew on traditions of participatory action research, emergent in technology-enhanced learning (Somekh 1997, 2001; Carmichael 2003), and on ideas about participatory design, drawn from computer sciences and software development (Olsson 2004). A further current came from project members' experience of international development projects and of participatory rural appraisal (Chambers 1994). Participatory action research offered a framing of project activities, including the development of an ethical framework, not driven by well-structured hypotheses but by dilemmas and challenges, explored with the aim of gaining a deeper understanding and improvement in practice (Muñoz and Jeris 2005, 8).

In the Ensemble project, data collection and interpretation processes informed by social and situated learning theories sit alongside discourse analysis and ethnography, and methods are blended and adapted to suit each as necessary. Elliott (2006, 178) suggests that action research methods should be chosen with the aim of helping practitioners to 'develop a reasoned capacity for action in the service of their educational values', bringing consideration of ethical issues into scope alongside other methodological deliberations. It is important to note that the methods and purposes of action research are themselves highly contested, and participatory action research is not the 'answer' to a clearly defined set of questions. Rather it needs to be understood as a set of particularizing and generalizing practices employed within multi-threaded project discourses.

A different perspective on 'participation' came from computer scientists who recognized in the Ensemble project a need to employ 'participatory design' approaches to software development and evaluation. Participatory design encompasses a range of approaches and 'degrees of user involvement' (Olsson 2004, 379) and has moved away from a simple empiricist view. There is increasing interest in the methods of social science, including action research (Gottesdiener 2002), and in integrating perspectives that reconstruct technologies as social practice (Suchman et al. 1999; Suchman 2007). This extends beyond gathering 'user requirements', to include exploration of the sense and use made of technologies once they become part of the social practices of different users, who are engaged as co-designers in developing both technology and practice.

Variability and adaptability are inherent to participatory research and more expansive versions of participatory design, and make it hard to predict potential issues for the purposes of ethical review. Brydon-Miller and Greenwood (2006, 119) describe action research projects as 'open-ended, collaborative, methodologically eclectic, and without specific methods, processes, or final goals determined in advance' and suggest that this makes it hard to review and evaluate ethical aspects of research plans at early stages of project development. Our commitment to engage participants and to allow them to contribute to the framing of research questions and technological developments necessitated a flexible ethical framework, developed through processes of formative critique from different disciplinary perspectives, and from the participating teachers and students themselves. At the same time we had to address formal review processes not premised on such commitments and based on narrower conceptions and assumptions about methods, roles and relationships, and what counted as successful project outcomes.

We were concerned that our commitments were not inhibited by a culture of ethical review that might restrict emergent research practices on the grounds of the potential for unexpected ethical issues to arise during research. We were also conscious that what might emerge from processes of co-design of research and participatory design of technologies would go far beyond the initial plans scrutinized as part of an ethical review process and that ethical approval would have no bearing on the actual practices that developed. This could lead to concern on the part of funding bodies, host institutions, participants and research users as to the quality of the research, and might compromise the project. We required a set of practices, processes and materials to serve as a guide and a 'stabilized' performance of project commitments, while being flexible enough to allow methodological, pedagogical and technological innovation and participant input.

In the remainder of this account, we discuss two aspects of our response to this challenge: (1) a specific 'enactment' of project commitments and approaches, developed to address the expectations of ethical review boards; and (2) a flexible and discursive approach to ethical practice which was employed in research settings. We characterize the latter as 'joint practical reasoning' which draws on Elliott's conception of participatory action research as the exercise of *phronesis* or 'practical wisdom'. It can also be seen as exemplifying Hall's 'culture of inquiry', where the focus is a developing ethical framework, broader than any specific enactment.

Ethical framework and ethical review

Discussions leading to a broad ethical framework and specific documentation required for the review process began even before the project commenced its funded phase in October 2008. The entire research team met over a period of several days and research ethics was a theme which was introduced and revisited regularly. In addition, related discussions about research settings, methods, research archiving, and publication strategies, for example, frequently involved a revisiting of ethical issues and consideration of whether the emerging ethical framework would need to take account of the issues under discussion.

Within the culture of inquiry, an ethical narrative emerged as one of the 'discursive articulations of practice' described by Hall (1999, 171). It proved useful for a member of the project team (one of the authors of this paper) to deliberately maintain this narrative by interrogating emerging plans based on prior experience of research and by offering 'plausible counterfactuals' (Hawthorn 1991, cited in Hall 1999, 158). These were 'what if' questions and scenarios which challenged the project's current understandings of its ethical practice, or to a research method which might raise issues about what constituted 'informed consent' or which generated data that might make preservation of anonymity difficult. Many of these issues arose from aspects of the project previously highlighted, including: the use of video and audio of classroom discussions – both whole class and small group working; the collection of online data generated as students interacted with online resources; and the potential for student learning opportunities to be affected (positively or negatively) by the use of new technologies. Some difficulties emerged where project objectives were in tension with each other or with established ethical commitments, for example the preservation of anonymity, attribution or informed consent. The project team had to reconcile the central role of data sharing (an intrinsic element of the semantic web's linked web of data) with commitments to data protection and privacy when these data were emerging from research settings. Similarly, the notion of informed consent had to be revisited where data was not simply being stored and retrieved for research purposes, but re-analyzed, repurposed and combined in ways not obvious or articulated at the time that consent was originally given. The ethical framework provided a framing for questions to be raised about how our use and development of advanced technologies might represent a challenge to our ethical practice and those of research participants, and a tool to encourage reflection as to how these tensions could be resolved. The formative nature of the discourse meant that questions were not couched in terms of 'would our ethical framework "cover" this?' Rather, the questions took forms such as:

- 'What do our ethical commitments mean for the way in which we need to introduce and potentially adapt this research method?'
- 'Are the notions of privacy promised by this technological system sufficient that we can offer them with confidence to participants?'
- 'Is our ethical framework as currently constructed adequate to deal with a situation in which …?'
- 'Are we sure that participants understand fully that this research method may have consequences in these areas …?'

The preparation for the process of formal ethical review was informed by these discussions, but also represented the discursive generation of an additional narrative. This seemed like a translated and 'edited' version of a richer account informed by and informing, critiqued by and critiquing, other project narratives and discourses, an important interface between our emerging understandings and plans and a more generalized notion of ethical practice.

The process of preparing for ethical review was complicated by conducting research in two universities. In one (Institution A) a university-wide ethics board sat at regular intervals and considered proposals for research by and within the institution. In the other (Institution B), responsibility for ethical review was devolved to faculty-level boards, each with its own processes and procedures. These differences were evident as we came to prepare the two sets of documentation for submission. We were conscious of producing material enactments of a wide range of practices which were in some cases still highly contested within the project and which had yet to be presented, negotiated and elaborated in different research settings – like 'snapshots' of our current state of understanding, underpinned by a number of key concepts and commitments.

In Institution A, a set of documents common to all research involving 'human subjects' required an abstract of the research, a section on the 'research protocol … to be used' and also included questions about the 'frequency of procedures'. For a research project only beginning to negotiate engagement with participants, these questions proved difficult to answer. In Institution B, a staged process was involved – the first involved our completion of a structured questionnaire designed to promote reflection on the part of the researchers, who were then asked to submit this with supporting documentation to a 'knowledgeable person of standing' identified by the faculty. The second involved a meeting and discussion, with the option of progress to a third stage with a full ethical review panel. The implications of certain responses for progress to further review processes was made clear, the accompanying notes reading:

> If you have [answered 'yes' to any of these questions] then you should assume that further discussion involving Stage 2 procedures is required because some aspect of your proposed research is likely to be 'ethically sensitive'. In practice, many issues can be resolved at this stage ... if you have [answered 'yes' to one or more of questions involving potential stress to participants or medical procedures] Stage 3 clearance will definitely be required.

In both cases, we submitted not only the formal documents required by the institutions but the current version of the broader project ethical framework, sample documents to be distributed to participants and other project documentation. And in both cases, ethical approval for the project to proceed was given, Institution A's board asking for some clarifications about project oversight and resolution of disputes.

Following ethical approval the project team discussed the two processes and there was agreement that, while we were generally confident of the outcomes of the review processes, Institution B's structured process had been more transparent and that the preparation of the submission had contributed to our thinking about the ethical frameworks we might use. Not only was our collection of documentation and examples a material enactment of our own (emergent) research practices and discourses, the structured but transparent questionnaire was itself an enactment of the faculty's own collective experience of the conduct of ethically sound research. By framing at least the early stages of the process as part of a discourse rather than as 'approval' or 'clearance', it contributed formatively to the ongoing culture of inquiry of the project, aligning well with our own practices and with the processes by which our broader ethical framework had been developed.

That said, there were elements of the more generalized review process of Institution A which were clearly designed to promote reflection on the part of researchers, including an open question asking: 'What do you consider are the major ethical issues in this proposal?' There was discussion within the project as to what issues should be offered and how these should be couched, and given that we saw the issue of 'informed consent' as one of our major areas for discussion with participants it was felt appropriate to mention this. As one of the preceding questions asked 'How and when will [participants'] consent be obtained?' our response – that the obtaining of consent would be regarded, not as a once-and-for-all prior event, but as a process, subject to renegotiation over time – was supported with a copy of our full ethical framework and copies of the template for consent forms which had been developed for use in project research settings.

Therefore, the 'single discipline' review process of Institution B did encourage group discourse relating to appropriate educational research ethical issues, but this did not encompass the full range of concerns that an interdisciplinary technology-enhanced project may face. The broader ethical review of Institution A attempted to cover a wide range of disciplines or to be discipline-independent, which invited interdisciplinary thinking and discussion – but it was not framed as part of an ethical discourse. The challenge for ethical review boards may therefore be to integrate the approaches of these two institutions with questions that initiate discussion and reflection on ethical issues and practices, whilst remaining open and wide ranging enough to allow for interdisciplinary thinking.

Research ethics as 'Practical Wisdom'

These different processes of ethical review, combined with a recognition of the importance of personal experiences (both of engaging with ethical issues and of research practices which might raise them), enriched through working as an interdisciplinary group, led us to explore in more detail the relationship between two elements in our culture of inquiry: the *ethical narrative* and that of *participation*, outlined above.

In such an interdisciplinary project, with participants from widely diverse disciplines, it is unlikely that the research aims of all project participants will fit simply into either Elliott's (1978) characterization of 'educational research' (which aligns with participatory action research and involves the practical intention to realize educational values) or 'research on education' (which aspires to produce 'objective knowledge' about educational practice). However, it is important that researchers reflect on and share the aims and underpinnings of their research and the project as a whole, opening up opportunities for discussion about methodologies, practices and ethical issues. Thus project discussions in which ethical issues are regularly revisited are key to conducting ethical research and realising Elliott's 'ethically committed action'. Echoing but also extending our understanding of the 'culture of inquiry', Elliott (2006, 169) argues this is premised on 'disciplined conversation in which reasons for action are scrutinized, critiqued and modified' and connects this approach with the Aristotelian concept of *phronesis* as a distinctive form of ethically informed practical reasoning.

To possess practical wisdom in Aristotle's view is to be good at thinking about what one 'should' do, and involves a combination of understanding and experience that allows one to make judgements in new situations (Hughes 2001, 84). *Phronesis* is one of three principal intellectual virtues proposed by Aristotle (2000), the other two being *episteme* and *techne*. *Episteme* is classed as scientific knowledge of eternal and universal truths (Aristotle 2000, 105). In contrast, *techne* is translated as art, craft or skill: the ability to 'bring into being things that are contingent and variable' (Wiliam 2008, 434). *Phronesis* transcends both *episteme* and *techne* as it concerns the problem of acting rationally in situations that are contingent and variable (Wiliam 2008, 434), and therefore allows responses to complex situations encountered in interdisciplinary work.

Hughes (2001, 84) interprets Aristotle's concept of *phronesis,* which involves assessing each potential action in the light of the particular situation, as entailing the following requirements and actions:

- Ethical frameworks cannot prescribe actions, only principles for consideration. They lay the foundations for ethical practice but each new situation or research relationship requires re-assessment of those codes in the light of the circumstances.
- The implications for ethical review processes are that it is not possible to prescribe practical ethical solutions to all imagined future issues. Attempts to pre-empt all problems and their solutions could lead to synthetic and potentially irrelevant statements being made in review documentation.

In the context of the Ensemble project, this involved 'tailoring' the ethical framework to take account of particular settings and situations. In one research setting, student use of an online learning environment was automatically 'tracked', generating detailed data about their behaviour and interactions. While this had not been explicitly mentioned in the original ethical framework, this was extended and aligned with the project's general commitments to informed consent and participating students were made aware of this additional aspect of data collection.

Phronesis also requires an understanding of underlying moral principles and also the experience to use that understanding correctly, so:

- Ethical frameworks are not sufficient in themselves to prescribe actions. In order to make ethical decisions, you need to have enough experience of the potential outcomes to make a judgement about the best course of action.
- Having an interdisciplinary group of researchers with varying levels of experience can be used as a resource for making ethical judgements.

In one of the Ensemble project research settings, technological innovations were gradually introduced within small elements of an undergraduate course, rather than introducing a range of new and untested technologies more broadly. This was underpinned by a commitment on the part of both researchers and teachers to a 'duty of care' towards students and a desire not to put them at risk in a 'high stakes' learning and assessment environment.

Phronesis, according to Hughes (2001), also requires a combination of understanding and experience that is continually being enhanced through confrontations with different situations. In the context of interdisciplinary research, this means that:

- Researchers and groups can benefit from reflecting on and sharing their experiences of ethical issues and the outcomes of the actions put into place to solve them.
- The interdisciplinary working and the culture of inquiry which the project seeks to establish should see the diverse and developing experience of participants as a resource upon which to draw in addressing ethical issues, rather than as a barrier to understanding.

In the course of project activities, we initially attempted to gather data about students' case-based learning in one research setting by providing them with a range of ethnographic 'probes' for self-documentation (audio recorders, video and still cameras and diaries). Even with the full cooperation of students, the data collected offered limited possibilities for analysis. Learning from this, in a second setting, we approached students with the proposal that they be accompanied or 'shadowed' by a researcher who would collect data on their activities. We had previously assumed that students would be less willing to agree to this, but in fact they indicated that the presence of the researcher would, in fact, be less intrusive than the demands of self-documentation. This change in approach actually resolved one area of concern, namely whether the participating students would themselves carry out data collection with due regard for the project's ethical commitments, but at the same time, necessitated a further renegotiation of the ethical framework and informed consent arrangements in the light of the new research relationships in that particular setting.

A *phronetic* approach to educational research involves more than a broad commitment to collegiality or democracy, and an open and democratic approach to practising research does not necessarily imply consensus in the moral aims of conducting research. As Boser points out 'democratic intentions do not obviate the need for thoughtful examination of the ethical implications' of our research (2006, 14). So ethical issues need to remain open questions, revisited, as research practices, technologies and relationships develop, and thoughtfully reassessed in the light of new understandings. In Hall's terms, the other narratives (disciplinary, pedagogical and technological) should always remain capable of challenging ethical practices, just as they should be subject to scrutiny, critique and modification in the light of emerging ethical concerns.

Practical wisdom, interdisciplinary working and critique in research settings

We have alluded to a set of ethical 'materials' which have emerged from discussions, informed by prior experience and disciplinary perspectives, and which accompanied the more constrained and structured ethical review documentation. We conclude this paper with a vignette of project engagement in one research setting, describing some aspects of the ethical issues involved and highlighting the role of the context-specific, formative discourses in which researchers and participants have taken part.

The setting is a postgraduate course in one of the participating universities in which the complexity of the subject matter, and the interdisciplinary nature of the field (which draws on technology, business, management, law and politics), makes learning with cases the dominant pedagogical approach. Students with diverse backgrounds engage with a series of presentations, films and other resources before working in groups to solve problems presented by the teacher. The teaching and learning environment has, until now, used few technologies, so introduction of the semantic web technologies into this setting is necessarily proceeding slowly – the teacher and students prize the team working and face-to-face negotiation skills that will prepare them for future employment.

When project researchers first visited the classroom to observe teacher and students at work, it followed a series of discussions about the nature and scope of the project's involvement, expectations and issues of confidentiality and privacy. The student group were then given an opportunity to discuss these issues, and were presented with a leaflet about the project, a tailored copy of the project's ethical framework, and a customized consent form which they were given an opportunity to discuss with the teacher and researchers. The project's documentation includes a series of consent form 'templates' which set out in a clear format, for example, what data are to be collected, from whom and for what purpose. These templates are customized to reflect both the nature of the setting and the outcomes of these discussions with teachers and students (including the detailed cases outlined above). These were the original documents submitted to the ethical review boards but, once adapted, each setting and potentially each research encounter (interview, discussion or classroom observation) could have slightly different, context-sensitive material reflecting different (and changing) notions of informed consent.

Ethical issues, and particularly that of informed consent, are never taken for granted and are the subject of continuing discussion. What has occurred, however, is more than a 'customized' set of ethical practices enacted by the research team; adoption of a *phronetic* problem-solving approach means that the different disciplinary perspectives and varied experience represented offer not only creative solutions to dilemmas but are also a source of critique of the ethical framework itself, which continues to evolve as a result. These critiques come not only from within the project team; in the research setting we describe here, the teacher challenged the way in which we were conceptualizing *confidentiality*. We had considered confidentiality primarily in terms of protection of individuals' privacy but the teacher argued that given the business orientation of the course concerned and the fact that classroom contributions might represent privileged information and particular learning outcomes might mean competitive advantage, we needed to adapt and extend our understanding in this area. This led us to revisit not only data collection protocols but also our thinking about long-term storage of data and the incorporation of primary classroom data into publications.

A more complex relationship between the ethical, pedagogical and technological strands of the project's work also emerged in the course of discussions with students about the collection of video data. This is a necessarily brief summary, but it captures both the participatory nature of the project, the potential for unexpected developments and the ways in which the different strands and narratives of the project intertwine:

- Teachers and students agreed that researchers could collect video data of lectures and group work as students worked on cases; students who were reticent were reassured that the video was being collected for specific research purposes – fine-grained discourse analysis.
- By the end of the course, student curiosity as to what had been observed had evolved into a realization that the videos might be of value in supporting their own learning, either as records of lectures, as reminders of their own contributions, or as opportunities for 'vicarious learning' by observing others.
- The teacher was also interested and was increasingly reflecting on his own practice and on exploring how students worked in small groups, solving problems and introducing knowledge from different sources into discussions.
- The ethical framework in this specific example was renegotiated so that teacher and students were able to view the videos in a specially established secure online environment, with the agreement of all concerned. This negotiation was not an easy one and the implications were explored particularly carefully; the prior experience of project members of supporting secure online spaces and establishing linked ethical frameworks (Carmichael and Youdell 2007; Wilson et al. 2007) was particularly important and strengthened participants' confidence in the solution offered.

This vignette shows how a commitment to participation, and the *phronetic* principle of drawing upon both understanding and experience to decide how to act, facilitated a creative solution to a complex and emergent problem. At the same time, it demonstrates how a single narrative (technological, pedagogical or ethical) cannot adequately express or inform a situation in which an unforeseen affordance of a technologically enhanced research process contributed to changed pedagogical and andragogical practices. These entailed a new technological aspect to the learning environment and a renegotiation of associated ethical practices. These experiences, pedagogical, technological and ethical, are now available to the project researchers as they engage with other, different settings and can inform the next phase of engagement and ethical framing of research.

The online environment in which the teacher and students can engage with research data represents an enactment of ethical commitments as much as (and possibly more than) the preparation of documents for formal ethical review. The emergence of new practices and the construction of new knowledge in complex, interdisciplinary and participatory research environments can be enabled and supported if ethical practice in research is understood as a series of open questions which are continuously scrutinized and critiqued from multiple perspectives. Ethical review processes are most valuable if they are understood not as 'approval' or 'clearance' but as contributing to, or even initiating, formative and dialogic practice.

References

Aristotle. 2000. *The Nicomachean ethics.* Trans. R. Crisp. Cambridge: Cambridge University Press.

Austin, W., C. Park, and E. Goble. 2008. From interdisciplinary to transdisciplinary research: A case study. *Qualitative Health Research* 18, no. 4: 557–64.

Barry, A., G. Born, and G. Weszkalnys. 2008. Logics of interdisciplinarity. *Economy and Society* 37, no. 1: 20–49.

Berners-Lee, T., J. Hendler, and O. Lassila. 2001. The semantic web. *Scientific American Magazine,* May: 34–43.

Boser, S. 2006. Ethics and power in community-campus partnerships for research. *Action Research* 4, no. 1: 9–21.

Brydon-Miller, M., and D. Greenwood. 2006. A re-examination of the relationship between action research and human subjects review processes. *Action Research* 4, no. 1: 117–28.

Carmichael, P. 2003. Teachers as researchers and teachers as software developers: How use-case analysis helps build better educational software. *The Curriculum Journal* 14, no. 1: 105–22.

Carmichael, P., and D. Youdell. 2007. Using virtual collaboration environments for education research: Some ethical considerations. *Research Intelligence* 100: 26–9.

Chambers, R. 1994. Participatory rural appraisal (PRA): Analysis of experience. *World Development* 22, no. 9: 1253–68.

Dogan, M., and R. Pahre. 1990. *Creative marginality: Innovation at the intersection of social sciences.* Boulder, CO: Westview.

Elliott, J. 1978. Classroom research: Science or commonsense. In *Understanding classroom life,* ed. R. McAleese and D. Hamilton, 12–25. Windsor: NFER.

Elliott, J. 2006. Educational research as a form of democratic rationality. *Journal of Philosophy of Education* 40, no. 2: 169–85.

Gottesdiener, E. 2002. *Requirements through collaboration.* Boston, MA: Addison-Wesley.

Hakkarainen, K., T. Palonen, S. Paavola, and E. Lehtinen. 2004. *Communities of networked expertise: Professional and educational perspectives.* Amsterdam: Elsevier.

Hall, J. 1999. *Cultures of inquiry: From epistemology to discourse in sociocultural research.* Cambridge: Cambridge University Press.

Hawthorn, G. 1991. *Plausible worlds: Possibility and understanding in history and social science.* New York: Cambridge University Press.

Haythornthwaite, C. 2006. Articulating divides in distributed knowledge practice. *Information, Communication & Society* 9, no. 6: 761–80.

Hughes, G.J. 2001. *Aristotle on ethics.* London: Routledge.

Kokelmanns, J.J. 1979. Why interdisciplinarity? In *Interdisciplinarity and higher education,* ed. J.J. Kokelmanns, 123–60. London: Pennsylvania State University Press.

Muñoz, K., and L. Jeris. 2005. Learning to be interdisciplinary: An action research approach to boundary spanning. *Health Education Journal* 64, no. 1: 5–12.

Nowotny, H., P. Scott, and M. Gibbons. 2001. *Rethinking science: Knowledge and the public on an age of uncertainty.* Cambridge: Polity Press.

Olsson, E. 2004. What active users and designers contribute in the design process. *Interacting with Computers* 16: 377–401.

Patel, U., and N. Solomon. 2009. Conversations across research projects on simulation: Uncovering the new worlds of work, learning and technology. Paper presented at the CRLL Conference, Lifelong Learning Revisited: What Next?, June 24–26, at University of Stirling, Scotland.

Pollard, A. 2007. The UK's Teaching and Learning Research Programme: Findings and significance. *British Educational Research Journal* 33, no. 5: 639–804.

Rimpilainen, S., and R. Edwards. 2009. The ANTics of educational research: Researching case-based learning through objects and texts. Paper presented at CRESC Conference, September, at University of Manchester.

Shadbolt, N., T. Berners-Lee, and W. Hall. 2006. The semantic web revisited. *IEEE Intelligent Systems* 21, no. 3: 96–101.

Somekh, B. 1997. Classroom investigations: Exploring and evaluating how IT can support learning. In *Using IT effectively in teaching and learning: Studies in pre-service and in-service teacher education,* ed. B. Somekh and N. Davis, 113–26. London: Routledge.

Somekh, B. 2001. Methodological issues is identifying and describing the way knowledge is constructed with and without information and communications technology. *Journal of Information Technology for Teacher Education* 10, nos. 1–2: 157–78.

Strathern, M. 2004. *Commons and borderlands.* Wantage: Sean Kingston.

Suchman, L. 2007. *Human machine reconfigurations: Plans and situated actions.* Cambridge: Cambridge University Press.

Suchman, L., J. Blomberg, J.E. Orr, and R. Trigg. 1999. Reconstructing technologies as social practice. *American Behavioral Scientist* 43, no. 3: 392–408.

Tscholl, M., F. Tracy, and P. Carmichael. 2009. Case methods, pedagogical innovation and semantic technologies. Paper presented at EC-TEL Conference, October, in Nice, France.

Wenger, E. 1998. *Communities of practice: Learning, meaning and identity.* Cambridge: Cambridge University Press.

Wiliam, D. 2008. Comments on Bulterman-Bos: What should education research do, and how should it do it? *Educational Researcher* 37, no. 7: 432–8.

Wilson, A., S. Rimpilainen, D. Skinner, C. Cassidy, D. Christie, N. Coutts, and C. Sinclair. 2007. Using a virtual research environment to support new models of collaborative and participative research in Scottish education. *Technology, Pedagogy and Education* 16, no. 3: 289–304.

Fieldwork for language education research in rural Bangladesh: ethical issues and dilemmas

M. Obaidul Hamid

School of Education, The University of Queensland, Brisbane, QLD 4072, Australia

This contribution documents the author's lived experiences in his fieldwork for his PhD research in the field of English as a second/foreign language in a familiar social setting in Bangladesh. The account suggests that insider researchers can helpfully draw on their tacit knowledge of local social and cultural norms and values to understand their research participants and their experiences, and behave with them in socially and culturally appropriate ways. However, it also shows that the insider perspective is more complex and problematic than is commonly assumed. To what extent local researchers are true insiders is questionable, particularly if they have social status differences with their research participants and, more crucially, if they are trained in Western academia and Western ethical norms. The major focus here is on the relevance of the ethical codes emphasized by the ethics committee of an Australian university to fieldwork in rural Bangladesh. The discussion that follows highlights personal ethical dilemmas, which resulted from an irreconcilable gap between the expectations of research ethics in Western academia and cultural realities and behavioural norms in the developing society. Implications of these ethical issues for fieldwork in developing countries as well as for institutional review boards are suggested.

Introduction

It is common for scholars and researchers from developing countries to pursue higher degrees in research in Western academia. Often these researchers, particularly in the social sciences, humanities and education fields, base their research on fieldwork in their own societies. This 'insider' perspective, as is commonly suggested, may help to avoid cultural, ethical and also epistemological concerns associated with research conducted by Western researchers (i.e. the 'outsider' perspective) in developing countries (see Smith 1999). However, the insider perspective is also susceptible to ethical questions that are related on the one hand to researchers' identities and the ethical orientation of their research in Western academia, and local norms of social and cultural behaviours and the absence of institutionalized research ethics in their societies on the other. To date these issues have received far from adequate attention in the literature.

I highlight here ethical dilemmas faced by insider researchers and invite discussion by presenting an experiential account of fieldwork in my own country, Bangladesh. With this end in mind, I discuss the relevance of the ethical codes emphasized by the ethics committee of an Australian university to the context of my fieldwork in rural Bangladesh. The discussion highlights personal ethical dilemmas, which resulted from an irreconcilable gap between the expectations of research ethics in Western academia and cultural realities and behavioural norms in the field. The contribution is divided into three sections. First, I introduce my research and its goals, and the specific social context in which it was located. Second, I position myself in relation to this research and its social context. This section emphasizes the problematic nature of researcher identity and offers a critique of the insider–outsider dichotomy. In the final section I relate a number of incidents from my fieldwork, which best reflect my ethical dilemmas and, consequently, my vulnerability as a fieldworker. I describe the implications of my experiences in the conclusion.

The research and its setting

The PhD study

Fieldwork played an important part of my PhD study at the University of Queensland in Australia (Hamid 2009). Using mixed methodologies, I investigated the relationship between Year 10 students' social biographies and their academic achievement in English in a rural sub-district in Bangladesh. The quantitative phase of the study involved two major instruments of data collection: (1) a questionnaire survey which elicited information on different aspects of the students' family economic, cultural and social capital and their *habitus* (i.e. the students' attitudes, motivation and other dispositional characteristics); and (2) an English proficiency test. The qualitative phase included selective student (n = 14), parent (n = 10) and teacher (six English teachers and six head teachers) interviews. I limit my discussion to student and parent interviews. Student interviews focused on students' attitudes, motivations, English-learning experiences, future education plans and career goals, and their perceptions of the influence of their family situations on academic achievement. The parent interviews elicited information on parental perceptions of the importance of education and English learning for their children and parental involvement in children's schooling and academic achievement. For cultural, ethical as well as practical reasons all interviews were organized in the homes of students (see Hamid 2009).

Nadiranga

The study was situated in a rural, peripheral sub-district called Nadiranga (a pseudonym) in northern Bangladesh, a South Asian nation of 160 million Muslim-majority people. Nadiranga with a population of 115,000 is one of the poorest sub-districts in Bangladesh (Hamid 2009). The literacy rate of the people aged seven and over in Nadiranga is 33%, compared to the national literacy rate of 45%.

Nadiranga is situated 500 km from the Bangladeshi capital, Dhaka. The sub-district has a rural, agricultural base with a small central town, in which are located the local government headquarters, a market place, three colleges and two secondary schools. Ten other secondary schools exist in more remote areas of the region, in addition to 116 primary schools, which offer free education to children up to Year 5.

Poverty and under-development characterize the socio-economic profile of Nadiranga. The famine which took place in Bangladesh in 1974 (after the nation's independence from Pakistan in 1971) was experienced most severely in Nadiranga. This human disaster gained international attention from donors and agencies that set up non-governmental organizations (NGOs), such as the Switzerland-based Terre des Hommes (locally known as *Chhinnamukul*) and Rangpur Dinajpur Rehabilitation Services (RDRS), to run rehabilitation programmes in the area for starving children. Dozens of NGOs, funded by government and international agencies, were operating micro-finance, health and sanitation, non-formal education and livelihood programmes at the time of my fieldwork in the last quarter of 2006.

Challenges in researching English language education in Nadiranga

The focus of my research was the teaching and learning of English in Nadiranga. I developed an interest in understanding the social circumstances and academic experiences of low-income and disadvantaged students in Nadiranga as a result of my own experience as a child, having been rehabilitated in Chhinnamukul from 1977 until 1987 along with hundreds of other children. Towards the end of my stay at the rehabilitation centre, I saw first-hand that my fellow rehabilitees were not able to continue their schooling once they were sent back to their homes, as their impoverished and uneducated parents could ill afford the educational expenses. After I left Chhinnamukul permanently, I continued my education although I was forced to earn my own living and educational expenses. I gained valuable insider experience, and after two decades my PhD project provided an opportunity to investigate the English learning experiences of students in Nadiranga in relation to their social backgrounds.

English came to Bangladesh in the wake of British colonial rule. It is widely believed to be a language of power, prestige and social mobility which is required for higher education and employment in the country. Bangladeshi state policies have made English compulsory for Year 1–12 students throughout the country (see Hamid, forthcoming). I was interested in investigating whether and to what extent poorer students from a rural region such as Nadiranga could utilize the benefits of English learning to ensure their economic and social mobility in a competitive society. The appropriateness of the teaching and learning of English in socio-economically disadvantaged regions such as Nadiranga might invite ethical questions, particularly when one takes into account the issues of limited resources and spending resources on priority areas such as poverty alleviation or literacy development in the first language (see Bruthiaux 2002). However, discussing ethics in relation to English language education in marginalized societies is too broad and complex an issue to be incorporated into the scope of the present contribution.

I had anticipated several problems for the fieldwork in a familiar social setting. First, Nadiranga had gained the reputation of being 'aid-dependent' and its consequences continued in the mindset of local people. I held concerns that my research could be misconstrued as being commissioned by an international aid agency and would result in a development programme for the socio-economic benefit of local residents. Indeed, when I was making copies of my survey instruments in a local copy shop during my fieldwork, the shop owner (who did not know me) remarked that I must be working for an NGO. His observation was understandable given the number of NGOs operating in the locality and the extent of fieldwork carried out by NGO workers and activists. Fieldwork for educational research was unknown in this locality and one of the challenges I anticipated was how to communicate to the local people that fieldwork could be carried out for independent educational research and, more importantly, that not all fieldwork is commissioned by aid agencies. I was unsure whether or how this issue was relevant to the Ethics Committee of the University of Queensland. Therefore, I did not elaborate on this issue in my application for ethical clearance. However, this was a crucial issue in my judgement. Fortunately, at the end of my fieldwork I was pleased that the local people did understand and appreciate the nature and purpose of my research which became widely known in the locality.

The second challenge was related to my identity and its implications for research and fieldwork. I was born and raised in Nadiranga. Although I left Nadiranga for higher studies and employment, I remained connected to the locality through regular visits to my parents, relatives and friends. I was well-known in the region first as a 'high-achieving' student and later as an academic at the University of Dhaka. I was the only person to embody that professional identity in the region. My new identity as a researcher was added to these established identities, which invited ethical questions. As Sikes observes:

> People considering embarking on insider research have to think very carefully about what taking on the role and identity of researcher can mean and involve in a setting where they are normally seen as someone else with particular responsibilities and powers. (2006, 110)

I had anticipated that my professional identity and its valuation, particularly in a disadvantaged region, would create social distance between me and my interviewees. In hindsight, this identity had an impact on my interactions with different groups of participants in complex ways. For instance, I was addressed as 'Sir'[1] by the majority of student interviewees. It is interesting that these students gave preference to my professional identity and muted my local identity in our conversations. The remaining students did not use an address form. Is it plausible that these students preferred my researcher identity (distant and objective) and considered me an outsider? In comparison, the English teachers whom I interviewed accepted me 'as one of them', although this may have been tempered by a misunderstanding of my professional identity with possible connections to the central education authority in Dhaka, and could have made them cautious of expressing their views on English teaching in schools. I suggest that it is irrelevant whether researchers claim an insider or outsider perspective. What is important is to identify to which of our multiple identities our participants refer at a particular moment, and to recognize that not all participants may refer to the same identity.

Although claiming an insider perspective is common in the description of researchers' relationships with their research and/or their social contexts, this position-taking can actually be more complex. Apparently, I had good reasons to claim an insider perspective. I was a member of the local community by virtue of birth, upbringing and permanent home address.[2] Unlike many researchers in developing societies who belong to the local elite (see Rizvi 1993), I was born into a lower-class family and as such could claim affinity with the students and parents with whom I worked. My class- and self-consciousness enabled me to empathize with my student interviewees who expressed a strong desire for social mobility through education but felt constrained by economic necessity. Nevertheless, I questioned whether I could really claim to be an insider in Nadiranga. I had left the area

20 years earlier, the locality would have changed substantially over time, as had my own values and outlook. I studied English literature at university which brought me closer to the values of British society, and later moved to Australia to study, where my orientation changed again to research and ethical norms of Western academia. Could I still claim to be an insider in Nadiranga simply because of birth and upbringing?

Making sense of Western research ethics and ethical dilemmas

Before I could start my fieldwork in Nadiranga, I had to apply for ethical clearance from the Ethics Committee within the School of Languages and Comparative Cultural Studies at the University of Queensland. The Committee emphasized the principles of informed consent, privacy, confidentiality, anonymity, participants' right to withdraw from research and avoiding harm to 'vulnerable groups' (children, in the case of my research, who were aged 15–16 years). These are standard ethical codes which are more or less common to institutional review boards (IRBs) in Western academia (see Israel and Hay 2006).

Given that my application for ethical clearance was in a prescribed form which contained a fixed set of Western ethical issues previously noted, I found myself in a situation where I was forced to view the social, cultural and ethical questions in Nadiranga through the prescribed ethical criteria. I was required to conform to these criteria for the sake of my research and the research degree towards which I was working. Said differently, I felt more concerned about research ethics *in theory* (i.e. in the application) than *in reality* (i.e. in the field). I had conversations with my fellow PhD scholars in social sciences and education who had already obtained ethical clearance for their research. I came to understand that they had similar experiences when they worked on their ethical clearance applications.

This engagement with the ethics in theory, which to some extent compromises ethical concerns, in reality is required for successful ethical clearance application.[3] Nevertheless, it was difficult to satisfy the Ethics Committee which required that I revise my application, although not substantially. The issues raised by the Committee were mostly related to language, style and conventional expectations of ethical clearance application with which I was not sufficiently familiar on account of my inexperience and inadequate socialization. More importantly, the Committee raised issues concerning the socio-cultural appropriateness of some fieldwork documents in terms of language and discourse:

> A few of the committee members feel that the consent and information sheets are overly wordy and not necessarily socio-culturally appropriate. The committee requests that you consider more user-friendly and simple language for your information packet. It is important to create documents that can be genuinely read, understood, and signed. At present some members feel the wording is too dense …[4]

The emphasis on simple and user-friendly language conveyed through this feedback is generally appreciable. However, the judgement that the documents were 'overly wordy' and 'not necessarily socio-culturally appropriate' was based on Western modes of discourse and communication, although implicitly it was assumed to be universal. Conventional expectations of written communication in Bangladesh are different from those in the West. In government departments letters from the public are expected to be verbose. Anecdotal evidence shows that letters sent to government offices can be returned to their writers if conventional expectations of format, content and the degree of formality or verbosity are not taken into account. Since the two documents in question along with the application for gatekeeper permission (see the discussion that follows) had to be submitted to central education authorities in Dhaka, those social expectations of written communication were taken into consideration while drafting them. Interestingly, documents prepared by a local researcher for local use were judged 'socio-culturally inappropriate' by a non-local IRB who had little knowledge of the society or the culture in question.

In addition, the committee's feedback had implications for translation in ethics clearance application. I had noted in my application that the two documents would be translated into Bangla[5] which was the dominant language of communication in Bangladesh. Although the documents were found dense and verbose *in English*, they might not be necessarily so *in Bangla*. This was not taken into consideration in the Committee's feedback. What are at issue are the questions of language and social reality as well as Western modes of discourse and communication; IRBs can be guided by a monolingual (English) view of the world.

Revising my application in the light of the feedback, I eventually obtained provisional ethical clearance for my research and was advised by the Committee to obtain gatekeeper permission from educational authorities in Bangladesh for final clearance. I applied for this permission from the Directorate of Secondary and Higher Education (DSHE), which reports to the Ministry of Education of the Government of Bangladesh. In Bangladesh bureaucracy is slow, and intervention is often sought. I requested approval from the official responsible in person and obtained an official letter of approval in two weeks. Importantly, the authorities did not offer comment or raise concerns about the fieldwork on ethical grounds. Either the Bangladeshi authorities were satisfied with the ethical clearance from the Ethics Committee of the University of Queensland or they were not concerned about ethical issues in educational research. In the absence of any ethical prescriptions from the DSHE, I was bound now only to abide by the principles prescribed by the Australian IRB. However important in theory, many of these principles either did not make sense or were impossible to abide by once I started my fieldwork. I will demonstrate this with examples in the following pages.

Informed consent and right to withdrawal

The concept of informed consent requires that research participants be fully informed of the research, the nature and extent of their participation and their right to withdraw from the study at any stage of the research (Israel and Hay 2006, 61). Accordingly, I briefed student participants in groups about the research in their schools and requested their participation. Although I explained clearly that participation was voluntary, the students were not free in reality to decide whether or not to participate because of: (1) my professional and local identity, and (2) the obligation created by head teachers in asking for the students' full cooperation. As to (1), probably the students could not refuse a university academic who was a former student of one of their schools and who was researching *their* experience in English learning in Nadiranga. With regard to (2), showing respect and obeisance to (head) teachers is socially binding for Bangladeshi students. All students from whom I requested participation in the eight schools in Nadiranga instantly agreed to contribute to the study. Whether or not their participation was voluntary could not be ascertained.

Once the students verbally agreed to participate in the study, I handed them the participant information package along with consent forms for them and their parents to sign. The consent forms were returned with student and parent signatures by the deadline agreed. However, it remains unclear whether parents were fully informed of the research by the information package. This was the case particularly with parents of little or no formal education who may not have comprehended what was involved, and may have been persuaded to sign the consent forms by their children. In the case of parents without the ability to write their names, the children themselves might have signed the forms on their behalf.

From a different perspective, however, informed consent is not an issue in a social context like Nadiranga where being able to participate in the work of people with higher education is considered an honour bestowed upon those who participate. For many students and parents the invitation to participate in the research was an opportunity to help a university academic (who also belonged to the local community) and therefore there was no question of non-participation. In fact, failure to participate could mean loss of opportunity. For instance, I selected only small samples of students from three schools for pilot testing of my survey instruments. In one of these schools a few students who were not selected asked me why I had deprived them of the opportunity to participate. My explanations of the purpose of the pilot test did not prove convincing, and their understanding was that they had been denied an experience that their friends alone would be able to relate to family and other locals.

The problem of exclusion arose again on a larger scale when I began working with students on the questionnaire survey and English proficiency test. For resource and time constraints I planned to work with selected secondary schools in Nadiranga. A few schools were excluded when the criteria of school location and gender of the student population were considered. One day I met the headteachers of two of the excluded schools in the marketplace who enquired why I decided not to work in their schools. They informed me that their students were aware of my research and had requested that I be invited to work with them as well. I explained my research constraints and was able to convince the headteachers why I could not work with students in all schools. Even then I had to offer assurances that I would visit their schools and talk to students, although they were not going to be my research participants.

The home setting and issues of hospitality, politeness and obligation

As previously noted, the students and their parents were interviewed in their homes for social, cultural and practical reasons. Ethical issues arising from fieldwork in the home setting have been discussed by Yee and Andrews (2006). These researchers pointed out identity conflicts in the home setting – between a professional researcher and a guest – since they had to suppress their researcher identities and act as proper guests. My fieldwork with students and parents in their homes presented similar conflicts. However, in my case the ethical issues were more complex than those suggested by these researchers.

For the majority of the interviews, I visited the homes and requested appointments with the parents and students. With a few families, I was able to request an appointment by mobile phone.[6] When I spoke to the father of one female student, one of the few wealthy men in Nadiranga, and asked for an appointment, he agreed on one condition: that I interview him and his daughter and have lunch at his residence. His condition placed me in a difficult ethical situation. On the one hand I wanted to conduct the interview in order to understand the economic, social and cultural capital that was invested by the family in the schooling and academic experiences of this high-performing student. On the other hand, as a researcher I was hesitant to accept the invitation as it would mean much time and effort on the part of the family. I attempted to avoid accepting their hospitality as politely as possible, but the father was insistent. Finally, I relented and accepted his luncheon invitation as well as his consent to the interviews. Although my researcher self was not entirely happy with the resolution, I justified myself on several grounds. First, it was important that I interview the daughter and the father of this wealthy family. Second, although the lunch was going to cost the family in terms of time, effort and money, at least money was not a concern. I decided to take some local sweets, the most appropriate gift to take on such occasions. However, the crucial reason for not declining his invitation was related to my insider identity. He was a socially distinguished man and as such deserved my respect and obedience. Saying 'no' to him (or to any person of his standing in Nadiranga) would be interpreted as conceit based on my professional academic and researcher identity, which I could not allow. I admit I could not hold fast to my researcher identity, and not at the expense of my other identities associated with the place of my birth.

Interviewing students and parents from poor and disadvantaged families also presented ethical dilemmas. Bangladeshi people, particularly in rural areas, are very hospitable and offer food to their visitors, whatever the purpose of their visit. A show of hospitality to me was predictable particularly as I was a familiar person in the locality. Moreover, I was considered 'a role model' for their children seeking social mobility through education. Almost all the homes I visited for interviews offered me food; some provided light refreshments while others substantial meals. Although I tried to reciprocate by bringing local sweets, I felt uncomfortable, particularly in those homes where it became clear to me that spending even a little extra money on food was a sacrifice on their part given their socio-economic status. However, I could not refuse the food offered to me. I was aware that doing so would send an inappropriate message: that I considered the food not good enough for my (recently achieved) social standing.

Privacy and confidentiality

The concept of privacy as defined in Western academia was not applicable to the context of my fieldwork in the home setting. The homes of the poor students and their parents where the interviews took place cannot be called 'private spaces' in the sense used in the West. Their dwelling places were open to their next-door neighbours, friends and relatives. Most of the houses (made of bamboo, thatch and corrugated iron sheets) are so close to one another that a neighbour can hear everything that is said in the house next door. My conversations with interviewees would have been audible to neighbours. Consequently, privacy and confidentiality of the views expressed by the interviewees could not be maintained.

The confidentiality of the views of interviewees was affected in yet another way. The interview was a special event for the family and their next-door neighbours. Although it was arranged inside the house, once I started conversations, I found that we were being observed by other family members and neighbours. Yee and Andrews encountered the same problem in their fieldwork in the home setting and found it 'impossible to identify beforehand who will be present at the interview' (2006, 408).

In the West this would be considered a breach of privacy and confidentiality. However, I felt helpless to do anything. Did I have the right to ask people to leave and let us continue conversations in private? No, I did not. I myself was an outsider in the house. I could not ask them to leave, although allowing them to stay and listen to my interview was a breach of privacy, both morally and ethically.

Although these incidents demonstrate the breach of privacy and confidentiality of the views of the interviewees from the Western perspective, this was not considered so in the context of the fieldwork. The people I interviewed had lived their entire lives in privacy-deficient environments. There was nothing wrong with entering a neighbour's house without permission. In fact, asking for permission would be considered unusual. Similarly, their conversations with an outsider (the researcher) would not be considered private or confidential in their judgement; it was a public event and therefore accessible to other family members and neighbours. It was probably unfathomable to them how one of them (the interviewee) could hold private conversations with someone (the researcher) who was not one of their family members or neighbours.

Occasionally, privacy had to be sacrificed for the sake of social and cultural appropriateness. Being a male adult it is socially and religiously inappropriate to interview a female student by myself inside the house. Therefore, I was required to request a parent or sibling to be present while I conducted the interview. Doing so was to compromise the privacy of her views, but not to do so would have compromised social norms of appropriate behaviour. This example clearly demonstrates that despite the ethical requirement to adhere to the researcher's identity, an individual's other identities (gender in this case) and their implications for fieldwork cannot be ignored or superseded.

In sum, the hegemony of Western academia assumes that the concepts of privacy and confidentiality are universal. In reality, however, they are not, as I have discussed in relation to my fieldwork. Western approaches to ethics are based on an individualistic view of society which does not characterize many societies in Asia or Africa. These societies, in general, view individuals as closely integrated into community and social networks. Therefore, the concepts of self and 'other' and related notions of privacy and confidentiality as applied to research ethics in Western academia appear significantly different, if not entirely irrelevant, in these societies.

Avoiding harm

The ethical requirement of avoiding harm to my Year 10 participants and their parents proved problematic. The research, inspired by critical approaches to applied linguistics (Pennycook 2004), aimed at highlighting geographic and socio-economic differences in English learning opportunities and their consequences in the Bangladeshi society. Asking students about personal and experiential issues evoked unhappy experiences of meeting socio-economic challenges at this 'vulnerable' age. The inner struggles of the students surfaced during the course of interviews. Struggles existed between their desire for a better life through educational achievement and their frustration at the manifold constraints their social origins brought upon successful learning and academic achievement (Baldauf and Hamid 2009). For example, Afrin, a self-conscious student from a remote school whose parents had lost their lands to the river and were about to lose their home, observed that she held no expectations of her forthcoming school-leaving examination or her future education or career. She implied that it was meaningless to 'dream' about future education or career aspirations as she knew well her parents could not support her in pursuing those dreams. Sathi, whose mother headed their family after her father's death, wished to have an MA qualification in the future. However, she said, 'I wish, but it seems I won't be able to make it'. Her explanation was, 'Our family income is not adequate enough to maintain our family. How can my mother bear my educational expenses up to that level [MA]'? (Hamid 2009, 168). Similarly, Rajib, a young man who was responsible for his mother and siblings in the absence of his father who had gone to Dhaka in search of manual work, indicated his feelings of helplessness, his desire for a university education, and the reality of his socio-economic situation:

> R : Do you have a wish to go to university?
> Ra: Yes, I do ... But I am not sure if my dream will come true because of our economic problems. (Hamid 2009, 168)

The interviews did cause distress, however temporary, by requiring students to talk about their experiences of socio-economic marginality and their hopelessness in pursuing educational aspirations. The psychological impact of the interviews is undeniable in the case of Monir who recollected how his family's socio-economic condition had affected his self-determination:

> R : Do you get all the things that you need for your studies – for example, books, pens, papers and then, money for taking private lessons – from home?
> M : No, not as much as I need.
> R : What sort of problems is caused by this?
> M : Sorry?
> R : I mean you said you don't get all the things that you need. How does it affect your studies?
> M : Not getting the things affects my studies. It changes my mentality.
> R : Ok, what kind of change in your mentality?
> M : For instance, I need a book but I can't buy it, and it affects my studies. I can't prepare my lessons before I go to the class.
> R : Yes.
> M : That's why I feel bad and think about giving up my studies. In those moments I become upset and keep myself away from my studies. I suffer from tensions and agonies. (Hamid 2009, 164–5)

On another occasion the impact of the interview was dramatic and left me embarrassed. I was interviewing Mitun's father, who was a manual worker. When asked to explain his family contribution to his daughter's education, he expressed worry and frustration: his income was not enough even for regular family meals. It was beyond his means to provide Mitun with study requirements such as books and private tutoring. He was well aware of the importance of education and of English for his 15-year-old daughter. Although he wanted Mitun to continue her studies to secure a better future, he knew how little he was able to help her academically and financially. The interview reminded him of his 'failure' to fulfil this parental duty. Suddenly, he burst into tears and kept sobbing. I was ill prepared for such emotional moments and did not know how to respond. I remained silent and allowed the powerful emotions to subside.

It was difficult for me to wear the mask of a dispassionate researcher in the wake of the distress occasioned by the interviews. The helplessness of the students who belonged to my community called for the activation of a different identity – that of a counsellor and supporter. I deliberately took up the role of counsellor and friend to many of the young men and women whose hearts I was able to read having passed through similar experiences of distress in my struggle for social establishment. After each of the interviews I encouraged the students to carry on despite their struggles and encouraged hope in a better future. I offered myself as a source of inspiration, reminding the students that I was not unlike them at their age. In doing so, I abandoned my researcher identity and assumed the role of confidant and activist for educational reform to ensure a better future for the young men and women of Nadiranga.

Implications and conclusions

My experience in working with the students and parents in the peripheral, rural community in Bangladesh has implications for IRBs in Western academia as well as for ethical fieldwork in developing countries. The account suggests that insider researchers can draw on their tacit knowledge of local social and cultural norms and values to understand their research participants and make sense of the latter's thoughts, words and experiences. In addition, this knowledge enables these researchers to behave in socially and culturally appropriate ways with their participants in their fieldwork. However, as I have argued in this paper, the insider perspective is more complex than is commonly assumed. Not all local researchers are truly insiders because they may have social status differences with their research participants. Moreover, their training in Western academia with regard to research ethics and methodology raises questions about their insider identity in their own societies.

The absence of local IRBs for social and educational research in developing countries leaves local researchers necessarily accountable to their own conscience and professional ethics. In addition, there is a requirement that researchers follow the ethical principles prescribed by ethics review boards in their affiliated institutions in the West. As discussed in this paper, this creates a different set of ethical dilemmas for researchers as many Western ethical principles are not applicable to the social contexts of the developing world. Institutionalization of local research ethics is apparently a solution to the problem. However, if there are discrepancies between local and Western review boards in terms of the definition of research ethics and ethical rules, the question will be, which ethics review board to follow – the local or Western.

In the absence of locally institutionalized research ethics, IRBs in the West could take a more flexible stance in granting ethical clearance to researchers seeking to research their own societies. If the fieldwork is to be carried out in a Bangladeshi local context, for example, it is questionable why the fieldwork should strictly follow the prescriptions of an Australian IRB. Signing memoranda of understanding between institutions in the developing and developed world may be a good step towards devising common platforms based on negotiations with regard to ethics for social and educational research.

The experiential account presented lends support to the contention that IRBs in Western academia may not fully prepare researchers for the unexpected in the field in developing societies (see Gallagher, Creighton, and Gibbons 1995). Therefore, the unexpected is to be expected and should be 'thought over' (Wilson 1993) and handled locally and contextually with reference to appropriate social norms and professional conduct. The researcher should remember that adhering to an objective, dispassionate researcher identity, however desirable, is not always feasible.

Acknowledgements

I would like to acknowledge the contributions of Nanette Gottlieb, Roland Sussex and Richard Baldauf to my PhD research and of Jo Grimmond who provided valuable feedback on an earlier draft of this paper. Two anonymous reviewers of the *IJRME* provided useful comments and feedback which I have incorporated into the final version.

Notes

1. It is common practice in Bangladesh to address teachers as 'Sir' by students (and other people), even if the latter were never taught by the former.
2. Every Bangladeshi citizen has a permanent address which remains his/her address forever. My permanent address no longer exists because the home as well as my village was destroyed by the river. Even then my passport carries this address since it cannot be changed.
3. This is evidenced by the ethical dilemmas described and analyzed in this paper. Although I obtained ethical approval for my research and the fieldwork, I could not abide by the ethical prescriptions of the IRB when faced with real people and their economic, social and cultural values and givens.
4. Copied from the feedback of the Ethics Committee on my ethical clearance application in July 2006.
5. I had not enclosed Bangla translations of the documents because the Committee or the School did not have access to this language.
6. Bangladesh has made significant progress in spreading the mobile phone network throughout the country. Mobile phone numbers are treated as private and confidential information in the West. However, this is not so in Bangladesh, particularly in rural areas. One can easily obtain someone's mobile phone number from another person and make a phone call. The issue of privacy or confidentiality is not relevant here.

References

Baldauf, R.B., and M.O. Hamid. 2009. English, socio-economic disadvantage and ELT policy: Insights from rural Bangladesh. Paper presented at the 2009 Asia TEFL International Conference, August 7–9, in Bangkok, Thailand.

Bruthiaux, P. 2002. Hold your courses: Language education, language choice, and economic development. *TESOL Quarterly* 36: 275–96.

Gallagher, B., S. Creighton, and J. Gibbons. 1995. Ethical dilemmas in social research: No easy solutions. *British Journal of Social Work* 25: 295–311.

Hamid, M.O. 2009. Sociology of language learning: Social biographies and school English achievement in rural Bangladesh. PhD diss., Univ. of Queensland.

Hamid, M.O. Forthcoming. Planning for failure: English and language policy and planning in Bangladesh. In *Handbook of language and ethnic identity,* vol. 2, ed. J. Fishman and O. Garcia. Oxford: Oxford University Press.

Israel, M., and I. Hay. 2006. *Research ethics for social scientists: Between ethical conduct and regulatory compliance.* Thousand Oaks, CA: Sage.

Pennycook, A. 2004. Critical applied linguistics. In *The handbook of applied linguistics,* ed. A. Davies and C. Elder, 784–807. Oxford: Blackwell.

Rizvi, S. 1993. Fieldwork in a familiar setting: The role of politics at the national, community and household levels. In *Fieldworks in developing countries,* ed. S. Devereux and J. Hoddinott, 153–63. Boulder, CO: Lynne Reinner.

Sikes, P. 2006. On dodgy ground? Problematics and ethics of educational research. *International Journal of Research & Method in Education* 29: 105–17.

Smith, L.T. 1999. *Decolonizing methodologies: Research and indigenous peoples.* London/New York: Zed Books.

Wilson, K. 1993. Thinking about the ethics of fieldwork. In *Fieldworks in developing countries,* ed. S. Devereux and J. Hoddinott, 179–99. Boulder, CO: Lynne Reinner.

Yee, W.C., and J. Andrews. 2006. Professional researcher or a 'good guest'? Ethical dilemmas involved in researching children and families in the home setting. *Educational Review* 58: 397–413.

Researcher tales and research ethics: the spaces in which we find ourselves

Julie White and Tanya Fitzgerald

Faculty of Education, La Trobe University, Bundoora, Melbourne 3086, Australia

The tales we tell here focus on the ethical issues arising from our research practice with vulnerable young participants and those for whom research has been inextricably linked with European imperialism and colonialism. The importance of relational obligations, temporality and potential for a continuing narrative approach to ethical research cannot be underestimated, and accordingly we recount our experiences in order to highlight these obligations as well as ethical tensions that we encountered. Importantly, our tales and the underpinning theorization suggest that Human Research Ethics Committees (HRECs) 'perform' their duties and make decisions to a pre-ordained set of prescriptive standards that do not necessarily take into account the agency of vulnerable young people or Indigenous women.

Introduction

While education researchers routinely tell war stories of skirmishes with ethics committees, in this article we narrate two quite different tales regarding ethical practices evident in our individual research experiences that called for a level of genuine engagement and interaction with participants and negotiation of relationships that went beyond any boundaries or criteria formally set by the two HRECs involved. The first account, from Australia, explores a challenging moral dilemma. Despite approval from both university and hospital ethics committees, a significant issue arose within an educational study involving young people with chronic illness. This story illustrates the relationship between research ethics and narrative and points to the need for a new form of support for researchers. The second account is from New Zealand and illustrates the overt emphasis on prescribed sets of standards that serve to protect the institution rather than assist researchers to negotiate ethical processes and protocols with participants. In this article, we acknowledge the deeply complex, uncertain and fragmented nature of research and the tensions and paradoxes that arise primarily because of the ways in which access, consent and ethical approval are sought, as well as the context in which these decisions are made. The experiences that we recount highlight that while HRECs have established protocols and principles in order to derive a level of certainty from research, it is the very nature of these protocols and principles that imbues research, at least in our experience, with a level of uncertainty.

Drawing on the tales that we narrate, we suggest that there are a number of inherent limitations with/in ethics committees, and new processes are proposed.

Performing in spaces

As qualitative researchers, we have found ourselves working in research projects that raise quite different yet related concerns about the principles, processes and procedures surrounding ethical issues and HRECs. Firstly, in the study of vulnerable young people, two highly respected ethics committees have rigorously scrutinized the proposal prior to the beginning of the study, and considered minor amendments during the life of the project. However, when unanticipated ethical issues arise, the process is found wanting. Similarly, the conceptualizations about ethical research seem out of step with contemporary approaches to research, particularly those from education faculties. Education is more a field than a discipline, which draws on a range of research traditions. The work of Australian HRECs, based on three principles established in the USA (Belmont Report 1979), focused on ethical principles for biomedical and behavioural research: (1) respect for persons, (2) beneficence, and (3) justice. What remains intensely problematic to us is whether these principles continue to be relevant or appropriate for educational research. Or indeed, perhaps, another question should be asked – is this the best we can do?

In the second project that is outlined in the later section of this article, 'research' is a word that has conjured up feelings of exploitation and vulnerability for the participants. Yet at the same time we are sanctioned by HRECs to conduct research with vulnerable people such as Indigenous women precisely because we have convinced this committee, on paper at least, that the research has 'benefit', will do 'no harm', and that the findings will be disseminated as high-quality publications. Thus, from the outset, as researchers, we too perform to institutional expectations and standards and remain mindful that our conduct as researchers can be subject to audit, surveillance, and, in the event of a complaint, sanctioned. What we are suggesting here is that the space that researchers occupy is colonized by an audit culture that demands that our work 'counts' and that it reflects particular understandings of research and research outcomes. Or as Bauman (2000, 86) so eloquently questions, are we as qualitative researchers working in these spaces or 'worked out and about' by them?

The starting point, we believe, is to think deeply about these spaces, how they are constituted and how they might work. Drawing on two narratives that outline the spaces that we found ourselves in, we tease out a number of questions such as – what are the spaces that we occupied? What actions did we take within these spaces? How might we respond to and accommodate the spaces that participants occupy? Reflecting on our shared experiences and thinking more deeply about these spaces, we would suggest that it cannot simply be about understanding these spaces but surfacing these complex questions in order to expose these multiple, competing and contradictory spaces. In other words, acknowledging and asking these questions are more important than the certainty of answers (Bauman 2000).

Julie's story

While official approval for the large nationally funded education project was granted by both hospital and university ethics committees, a conundrum arose in the final year that did not breach any ethical procedure or requirement, but nevertheless was confounding. I worried over what I had been told and eventually wrote about the event in order to make sense of the experience and to decide the best way forward. Perhaps the best way to begin is with the facts of the case:

> Lanie is a 16-year-old girl who lives in a middle class Australian suburb and attends a selective-entry high school. She's academically gifted – particularly in mathematics. She is from a Chinese background and has an eating disorder and until recently attended weekly counselling sessions. She has been hospitalized on several occasions. She recently told researchers of her admission to a Chinese psychiatric institution for an indefinite period during 2008. After four months there she was considered cured as her weight and eating patterns were deemed normal, so she was permitted to return to her life in Australia.

This 100-word synopsis has the hallmark of traditional research writing. It is objective rather than subjective and provides a rational and reasonable summary devoid of emotion, opinion or interpretation. What's missing, however, from this account is any sense of the impact of this event on the young person. Nor are the researcher's responsibilities brought to the fore.

The psychological dimension of anorexia nervosa is generally acknowledged, and assumptions and judgements about those suffering from this condition are readily made inside and outside hospitals and schools. In general, the condition a young person has, together with their gender, age and place of residence is similar to the information we have in a passport (White and Hay 2005). It does give some indication about where a person has travelled but it tells you very little about their identity, and a core element of our study relates to identity. The research question we set out with is:

> What do young people who have experienced trauma or chronic illness articulate about themselves and their experiences in relation to education connectedness, identity, social relationships and experiences with professionals?

An excerpt from the interview where Lanie revealed that she had been hospitalized in China is included here so that the reader might vicariously experience how the story unfolded. Without the visual cues gained from watching her face or the nuanced way she emphasizes particular words and how her voice sounds, it is difficult, but I hope you get a sense of her matter-of-fact telling and our gradual realization of what we were being told:

> Okay, well I guess things have changed a bit because in 2007 my parents, like, I was being treated at X Hospital and my mum kind of told me we were going to Beijing for a holiday.
>
> *Yeah we remember that, just before then we saw you, we haven't seen you since then.*
>
> And it turned out that my mum wasn't happy with the treatment … because I hadn't been … like my mum reckoned that I needed to be hospitalized again but, like, my doctor said I didn't need to, so there was some conflict there and so my mum decided to send me back to China and she, like, hospitalized me.
>
> *In China?*
>
> In China

And you didn't know that was coming, did you?

I didn't know that was coming. And so ... I guess ... it's of relevance to your project? But not very happy ... for me, because I was hospitalized for four months.

In China?

Yes

Well why don't you just tell us that story if you want to ... that's amazing ...

It's awful, actually, but I guess it's relevant to what you're doing?

It certainly is. Sure is. As long as you're comfortable to go there, we don't want to make you traumatized.

I'm okay. No I'm okay because it's good to get it out. But basically I was being treated for anorexia, right? But my mum sent me to a mental clinic, like, a psychiatric ward. And I was in with people with, like, OCD and, like, screaming people and just, like, an entire hospital dedicated to, like, psychiatric ... and, like, so that was, like, and ... so, like, my mum just totally cut off connection with X, my doctor here and, like, she just ...

I had, like, one interview with the director of the ward and suddenly, before I knew it, I'd been tricked into going. I was told, like, I was going to have another session with her ... and they just hospitalized me straight away. That was quite awful and, like, in my opinion, not fair like considering she wouldn't let me be hospitalized in Australia, so I was really angry about that.

And, like, because here, there's like an eating disorder treating kind of plan and that really helps a lot, like. Over there, there wasn't any plan to treat. It was like, there was a head nurse there and, like, the head nurse has a lot of control compared to the nurses here. So what happened, like, the head nurse had actually had anorexia and bulimia before, so like there were about three or four 'eating-disorder' people in the children's ward and what she did ... she totally took us under her wing. And there was a lot of conflict between the doctor and the head nurse because she thought she knew how to treat us.

In my opinion, she had no medical degree or anything, but she thought she knew how to treat us. So she like took ... she took control of our eating plan and everything like that. And she would give us very capricious kind of random tests. She'd be, like, 'This is a fried bun, okay?' And what she'd tell the kitchen is 'Cut it into lots of pieces,' so that oil, like, so the entire thing gets fried, like, really, really well and she's, like, 'Eat this. If you don't eat it you're not passing the test.' Or something like that. And then she would, like, bring back pieces of fat meat and she would be, like, 'You need to eat this.' And, like, so the treatment was very different.

So, was she trying to say not necessarily you're going to want to eat this but you've got to do it and ...?

'You have to.'

Force yourself to? Even if it's something that you find repulsive?

Yeah, because basically, 'You have an eating disorder,'

'You need to gain this weight and you need to get over it so you're just going to eat this.'

'If you don't eat it, you're going to get bottle-fed.'

The interview transcript continues for another 19 pages. The purpose of sharing this excerpt is to provide some background so that the researcher's ethical responsibilities emerge and unfold for the reader.

At the end of the interview, my co-researcher and I headed to our separate cars to rendezvous at a café in a nearby shopping centre. We each sought assurance that we had heard correctly and kept going over and over what we had been told. We really did not know what to do with this information. During the next week I arranged for the recording to be downloaded, delivered and transcribed.

I could not sleep for several nights and continued to worry about what to do with this heavy weight I had taken up. During that first week I was distracted while going through the motions of everyday life, as I was consumed by what Lanie had revealed. Eventually, I sat at the computer in the middle of the night and began to write. I wrote to understand what I had heard in the hope that I might work out how I should behave, and what my responsibilities were. I just could not talk about it with anyone else, as it was too shocking and was not yet a coherent story. An uneasy feeling that I needed to report this as abuse took hold. But I had no idea whom I should talk with.

It occurred to me that I really needed to tell my research team about what Lanie had revealed, so I just came out with it in one meeting. My co-researcher was absent. While everyone looked a bit shocked, no discussion ensued and no suggestions were made as to how it should be addressed. One of the other researchers suggested very tactfully and gently, that I might like to talk with an ethicist, and offered to arrange it. I was most grateful for her serious attention to this issue, and the unresolved responsibility that still troubled me.

I met with the ethicist and my colleague a couple of weeks later and was surprised how much support she provided – particularly how she guided my thinking through my responsibilities. I was unsure what an ethicist might be like, but any preconceptions I brought with me were soon dispelled. I quickly left behind the feeling that I was going to be in some sort of trouble. The good sense of humour accompanied the sensitivity of counselling with the ability to unravel issues clearly and logically. The discussion about Lanie's experience and my responsibility ranged from the motivation of the parents and the pointlessness of demonizing them to the question of serving the interests of the young person above all else. I pointed out that I was a researcher and formerly a teacher and had no business involving myself in psychological and medical aspects of this youngster's life. Nor did I have credentials or mandate to interfere in her family and the accompanying cultural and political issues. I did visit Lanie one more time, even though this was not in the interview schedule. The discussion with the ethicist impressed upon me the importance of keeping the door open for future access to support for this young person even though her family had withdrawn her from the hospital programme. I left her with a list of counsellors and their contact details as well as relevant websites. While she looked bemused, I suggested she tuck it away somewhere as it might come in handy one day.

Tanya's story

> We asked you to work with us because we need your voice. If we get out there and talk about how we have to advocate for our *tamariki* (children), for our people and for our future we get known as 'radicals'. We're not, we know what we need to do but getting it done is hard. That's why we came to you. You have an understanding of *nga mea Māori*

> (things Māori) and we know you will listen and guide us get to where we want to be. (Aroha, NZ)

I have begun this section of the article with the invitation that was extended to me in 2002. This was not a project that originated from my own work and as the *korero* (words) above indicate, my role was to act as a catalyst for this research and to provide a 'voice' that could alleviate the silences around research for/about Indigenous women principles.

This invitation came from a group of *Māori* women school principals in Aotearoa New Zealand who wanted me to undertake a research project that documented their professional biographies and highlighted their experiences as educational leaders. The women were concerned that their narratives, experiences and particular challenges they faced were never explicitly or publicly discussed, at least in academic texts. Drawing on their own networks the *Māori* women extended invitations to Indigenous women from Australia and Canada to join the group. Initially a two-year project, we are now in our seventh year, and there are now 17 women in the group. As Barbara (Australia) explained:

> Getting you involved in this project is a form of co-option. You can create the space for our voices to be heard, for our views to come forth. I don't know the academic game. we need help … we need allies.

From the outset this was a project that was shared by us all. However, I remained intensely aware that while I was invited to act as a voice, my role was not to offer an authoritative voice. My voice was not the one of authority and nor was it my role to legitimate the voices of Indigenous women. In effect I was a *mangai* (mouthpiece) through which Indigenous women began to speak up and speak back to narratives that had, at this point, overlooked their voices. Here too I was mindful of Michele Grossman's (2004) critique of non-Indigenous women using text to re-inscribe relations of power, that is, the non-Indigenous researcher/writer acting as the 'knower' and locating Indigenous women as the 'known'. This is essentially the reason why this part of my lived experiences as a researcher appears to utilize a more distanced voice than my colleague, Julie.

I was acutely aware that I was not the authoritative voice in this project and that Indigenous women co-opted my voice and positionality. These were the spaces that we occupied; a space in which we confronted the relationship between us, negotiated how the research was to proceed and the reciprocity that emerged. This was a markedly different space to what was occupied by the HREC. This Committee, mindful of its own institutional role, was concerned that questions about process and protocol were confronted *before* the project proceeded whereas in this instance, Indigenous women wanted to engage in these discussions *during* the project. What was therefore worked over in the spaces between me as the 'other' and Indigenous women was an understanding that Indigenous women and their communities rightly occupied this space and that I was an invited participant. This space was thus oppositional to the HREC that gave permission to the researcher to position herself as authoritative and Indigenous women as participants. Put another way, in this space, I as the researcher could not, and did not claim, to be an expert or to have expertise.

Across (and beyond) this project what became important was the dialogue, the negotiation and re-negotiation of our roles, and our responsibilities not to the project *but to each other*. Barbara (Australia) alerted us all at one point that it was about 'us and you and me' [indicating self]. Although these discursive threads connected us as participants, they were inherently complex. Here I am reminded of Bhabha's (1994, 45) words that:

> The question of identification is never the affirmation of a pre-given identity, never a *self*-fulfilling prophecy – it is always the production of an image of identity and the transformation of the subject in assuming that image.

Despite anxieties that I had, such as whether this research should have been undertaken by an Indigenous researcher (Collins 1998; Cram 2001; Marker 2003; Menzies 2001; Moreton-Robinson 2000; Smith 1999), I was excited about the invitation and considered it a privilege to have been approached. It was, in my view, a unique opportunity to engage in a project that involved listening to and understanding the lived experiences of Indigenous women 'in and on their own terms' (Harding 1987; Smith 1999). From the outset this project recognized the power of the participants to invite access, shape the research direction and share the knowledge that was produced. In essence, the project was built on and recognized:

> our interconnection and inter-connectedness. We have told some of our stories and there have been some we have yet to tell. Maybe it isn't for us to tell them by ourselves, maybe we need you to listen … and we trust you to be truthful with our stories … we want you to be with us and know what it is that needs to be done. And because we have told you these stories we are now connected. (Jane, NZ)

The sole focus of the project was not to gather stories and re-tell them in productive and respectful ways. The relationship *between* us and our partnership transcended conventional research practices regarding data collection, analysis and reporting. That is, there was not the 'distance' between us; a distance that is generally and usually expected between 'researcher' and 'participant'. As I have argued before (Fitzgerald 2004), Indigenous women occupied powerful terrain primarily as *tangata whenua* (people of the land) and because of the knowledge that they possessed and chose to impart. Implicit too in Jane's *korero* (narrative) is an indication of a level of scrutiny by and accountability to those who told some of our stories that arguably inverted the traditional researcher–subject relationship (Harding 1987). Put another way, as a researcher I was accountable to these Indigenous women and their communities and while this did not subvert my responsibility to a HREC, it is my experience that the accountability exercised by Indigenous communities was more exacting than that which any HREC could demand.

Negotiating with/in the spaces

All research that involves human participants is subject to the scrutiny of institutional ethics committees. This does not, however, guarantee that research is pain free or that power relations between 'researcher' and 'participant' do not exist. Despite an increasing awareness by ethics committees of the complexities and difficulties of research for/with Indigenous communities, participation is painful and issues of access, control and appropriation remain (Smith 1999) as Shirley and Barbara lamented:

> I have been involved in research before. I did not really agree with what was being done but the researchers told us they had approval from an Ethics Committee. I didn't see how I could really say I did not want to be involved if some flash committee had thought the

> project was okay. But you know, and I still feel to this day that something was taken from us and nothing was given back. (Shirley, Australia)

> I felt that the white researchers swooped on in here, got what they were looking for and left again. We have not heard from them since, I have no idea what they have written and I have no idea what was supposed to have been achieved or gained from the experience. (Barbara, Australia)

In New Zealand research that is for/with/in *Māori* communities is subject to particular scrutiny and a particular set of questions as there is a degree of consciousness that Indigenous research can be subject to exploitative practices (Smith 1999). For example, one HREC asked for the following questions and issues to be addressed:

> Could your research involve Maori participation, either by deliberate selection or by random sampling? Could it impact on Maori, or be of particular relevance to Maori?

> If 'yes', please explain how your research process is consistent with the provisions of the Treaty of Waitangi. State what consultations and/or collaborations, and with which *iwi*/ group, have or will be undertaken. What involvement does this group have in the project? How will the results be disseminated to the consulted group and participants at the end of the project?

What these questions highlight is that the HREC is primarily interested in the role of the researcher, a certain level of objectivity and neutrality, the protection of the institution and the dissemination of knowledge at the 'end of the project'. Importantly, the HREC appears to work from the standpoint that priority for research involving 'Maori participation', or of 'relevance to Maori' originates from priorities set *by the researcher* or by inference, by a particular funding body. There is no questioning as to how the research project was devised, whose interests the project represents, only if it is 'relevant', 'consistent' and involves a level of collaboration. Thus, there is little or no recognition of the *active* and sustained involvement of Indigenous community and elders, the nature of the knowledge that is passed on and its sacredness, and little understanding of the active and contested nature of issues such as control and access in Indigenous research and the production of knowledge for/about indigenous communities. Presumably if any researcher can satisfy this HREC with his/her/their responses to the above questions, then consent for the project is forthcoming. Reading the above text against the grain, it would appear that this particular HREC is 'performing', that is, asking expected questions and requiring an expected response in order for consent to be forthcoming. There is a marked absence of the complex pedagogy of negotiation, dialogue and the dynamics of power and authority (Marker 2003). Furthermore, as authors we would like to recognize that these principles and the questions demanded by the HREC may appear to be puzzling for readers who may not be familiar with Indigenous communities. But what this demonstrates is institutional recognition for the *rangatiratanga* (sovereignty) of Maori and a commitment to Maori as *tangata whenua* (people of the land).

This was a project that had neither a defined starting point nor an endpoint. Although several further applications have been made to the HREC to extend approval for the research (an institutional requirement), the invitation to undertake this project and the access that was negotiated, as well as the reciprocity embedded in our relationship, in essence means quite simply that the principles negotiated *with/for/by* the Indigenous women do not have an endpoint. While institutional committees adhere to western views of a beginning point and an endpoint, the *kaupapa* (principles) and *whakawhanaungatanga* (relationships), that define how and what we did *does not cease*. Thus, any HREC that performs to a set of (western and westernized) principles and guidelines demonstrates not only a surface commitment to Indigenous research and associated ethical principles and practices but also a public misrecognition of Indigenous research itself. Should it be the case that consent originates *from* an ethics committee or that an ethics committee should receive consent *from* the Indigenous community? The latter has the potential to locate indigenous communities as powerful in the research process, not the HREC. What then might be the long-term consequences if researchers were accountable to indigenous communities for their conduct, reciprocity and the knowledge that was negotiated?

My experiences in this project have highlighted for me that respectful research that values the interests of indigenous communities and peoples *must* take precedence over institutional claims to protection, objectivity, neutrality and defined project deadlines. I remain accountable to the Indigenous women and their communities for the knowledge that I gained and the knowledge that I produce. As I have noted elsewhere (Fitzgerald 2004) the ethics principles and practices that underpinned this project did not begin with an ethics application, but in dialogue with Indigenous women. Questions that were raised included:

(1) What are the expectations of Indigenous women regarding this project and its process?
(2) What is my role and how can I meet my obligations to participants and their communities?
(3) How might this research be conducted and proceed in a respectful way?
(4) How might the interests and values of Indigenous communities take precedence over institutional demands?
(5) How can cultural ownership of knowledge and treasures be assured?
(6) Whom are we accountable to for the research and its outcomes?
(7) In what ways can I contribute further to the professional work and activities of Indigenous women?

These are, and remain, serious questions that bring into sharp relief the critical nature of the relationship *between* participants and the negotiation of all aspects of the research and its outcomes. The above seven questions arguably go beyond an affirmative reply to questions such as:

> Could your research involve Maori participation, either by deliberate selection or by random sampling? Could it impact on Maori, or be of particular relevance to Maori?

While the questions asked by the HREC place responsibility for the ethical conduct of the research directly on the researcher, the very nature of the questions relegates Indigenous peoples to the periphery as the principles they might wish to negotiate with a researcher have not been considered. By their very nature, HRECs have ritualized technologies and practices which are, as we have argued, derived from a set of principles and protocols that are deemed to be logical, rational, sequential, objective and pragmatic. However, as our lived experiences indicate, the pragmatic realities of research are that it is messy, ambiguous, contradictory and fragmented. Furthermore, standardized forms such as that which HRECs frame and use to make judgements about a project, situate participants as both objects and subjects of the research. This is antithetical to working with vulnerable young people and Indigenous communities and the net effect is that they are 'Othered' by the very processes and HRECs whose mandate is to 'protect' from 'harm'. Crucially too, any 'lack' of recognition of Indigenous peoples and Indigenous processes, particularly in Aotearoa New Zealand, is a form of re-colonization as Linda Tuhiwai Smith (1999) has powerfully argued.

What is critical then is dialogue and negotiation as the very first step in a research project and a connection between the researcher and participants that establishes a relationship based on reciprocity. In terms of the project that I was involved with, this process of negotiation established the *kaupapa* (agenda) for the research from inception to completion (and beyond) as Aroha, Barbara and April highlight:

> I think I may have got more out of our journey than you [researcher] have. I have been able to think about what I believe in and value and we know you have followed the *kaupapa* (plan) we set up with you. I think that we all honoured what we decided and we know that you will come back to us and keep telling us what is happening with your own work and writing. (Aroha, NZ)

> I was not convinced that this [project] would work. I thought you would take our words and we would hear nothing more from you or read about what we said, or your version of what we said, somewhere. This has not happened, not yet anyway. I guess it isn't going to happen because we now know you and at the end of the day, we can always rescind our approval for any more writing and our stories return to us. (Barbara, Australia)

> I knew this would work when you came along the first day to listen, you didn't do anything else – I expected notes to be taken, a recorder to come out, but no, you just listened. It's not about speaking; it's about listening and knowing then what to say if it is for you to say it. Over a cup of tea or the dishes we always listen as you never know what is going to be said or told to you and if you listen you can get it right. (April, NZ)

In terms of this project, there were a number of guiding principles that underpinned our *kaupapa*. Each of these principles was negotiated and originated from the participants. As the initial group increased in size, we returned to these principles; these were, in effect, our *kawa* (protocols):

(1) Approval for the research, research methods and research outcomes rests with the Indigenous participants.
(2) Research is a process of ongoing dialogue and collaboration between and among us.
(3) Develop and share understanding by looking and listening and find a place from which to speak.
(4) Acknowledge and respect individual community, language and *whakapapa* (lineage/family) each person brings to the relationship.
(5) Honour the knowledge that was imparted from the past, in the present and for the future.
(6) Act in a respectful, trustful and responsible way and understand the principle of reciprocity.
(7) Actively contribute to community through the research process and outcomes.
(8) Ownership of the knowledge and the process rests with Indigenous women and their communities (see also, Fitzgerald 2004).

The drawing up of these principles and discussions we had was a very painful reminder of what had occurred on previous occasions. As the voices of Shirley and Barbara indicate at an earlier point in this article, permission from an ethics committee for their involvement in previous projects with other researchers and research teams had rendered them powerless. Although the ethics committee may well have intended for principles to be acknowledged and adhered to by the researcher, the potential relationship with either Shirley or Barbara was minimized and colonizing actions surfaced (and remained). For both Shirley and Barbara, research was a colonizing space and their agency with/in space had been neither recognized nor acknowledged.

Contesting spaces

The HREC generated regime of truth making around what constitutes research ethics and ethical research is deemed to be objective and requires researchers to act and react in particular ways. The spaces that HRECs create (and defend) are so intensely woven into the fabric of institutional life that it is almost impossible to either contest this space or create another space. Institutional regimes are solidified by the codification of ethics principles and practices at a national level. In New Zealand, for example, national codes of ethics (for research as well as professional practice) exist in various forms depending on the discipline or the profession. The Australian Code for the Responsible Conduct of Research (Australian Government 2007) was jointly issued and publicized by the National Health and Medical Research Council (NHMRC), Universities Australia (formerly the Australian Vice Chancellors' Committee [AVCC]) and the Australian Research Council (ARC). Compliance with these ethical codes requires that guidelines, practices, protocols, pro formas, uniformity and mechanisms of surveillance exist to ensure and assure compliance. Adherence to these codes is designed to govern (and restrict) practice as well as impose regimes of institutional order that require researchers to think and act in particular ways. And a glance at a number of universities across Australia and New Zealand confirms the creeping managerialism that is evident, as HRECs are increasingly subject to surveillance through risk management policies and practices (see Halse and Honey 2005).

There is an abiding dissonance between research practices and institutional discourses surrounding research ethics. This is troubling and unsettling primarily because this dissonance exposes a rupture between the 'real world' of research and institutional practices that simultaneously define and territorialize what 'counts' as ethical research. What has occurred is a shift in emphasis by HRECs from a focus on those involved with the research as participants to an intense concern about the data to be collected and the limitation of liability for the institution (Halse and Honey 2005). Put simply, the gaze of HRECs has shifted from concern about researchers and participants to procedural processes to protect the institution. Accordingly, HRECs now engage in preventative policies and practices that are designed to reduce the risk of 'harm' to the institution. This is their 'perfomative power' (Chiapello and Fairclough 2002).

As our two stories reveal, there is a disconnection between the technologies of HRECs and the 'real' world of educational research. What these stories further highlight is that researchers cannot merely 'perform' research according to the textual affirmations required by HRECs. Although speculative, it is possible to suggest that had either of us conformed to the objectivity, rationality and truth embedded in statements required by HRECs; we would have been vulnerable as researchers to claims that we had acted in oppositional ways to the principles and practices that were shaped by our participants. It is simply not possible, in advance, to predict how participants might engage with a research project (if at all) or how the messy terrain of educational research might be encountered. There can be no 'moment of security or cognitive certainty' (Keenan 1997, 1), but the possibility does exist for researchers to adopt care and respect in their negotiations with participants.

While Allen et al. (2009, 139) suggest that ethics review shifts from 'a single bureaucratic moment' towards a continuously open and critical conversation within a community of researchers, we propose a more formal allocation of responsibility. A suitable process to support ethical and respectful research could include the appointment of resident ethicists or ethics ombudsmen and women. Unlike the 'research ombudsman' focused on policing researcher misconduct proposed by Vaux and cited in Ross (2008), we envisage the role as supportive and enabling, involving discussion of unfolded and unanticipated ethical concerns. The purpose of such appointments would be very different to the distant and feared HRECs whose focus is on researcher compliance and minimizing risk for universities *before* projects commence. Consideration of ethical issues arising *during* research moves discussions beyond ethics 'clearance' or 'approval' and heralds an approach more in keeping with the complex approaches to contemporary research.

Ethical decision-making and moral action are subject to negotiation by researchers and their participants, not by HRECs. By doubting the claim of authoritative knowledge forwarded by HRECs together with the privilege and power of this knowledge, we question their suitability for contemporary educational research. What we would like to underscore is that our lived experiences as researchers illuminate the complex, non-linear and competing spaces in which research takes place, spaces which researchers and participants occupy, although ostensibly on different terms and for different purposes. It is imperative that the institutional power of HRECs does not regulate these spaces but that genuine ethical research is conducted that permits researchers and participants to work productively within these spaces and to be supported by institutional processes.

Conclusion

What these lived experiences have highlighted for us is the importance of understanding how we as qualitative researchers are positioned in the spaces that we occupy, how we might position ourselves and how participants might also occupy these spaces *on their own terms*. Accordingly, we suggest that we need to think seriously about the spaces in which we find ourselves and doing this allows for the possibility that we can continue to inhabit and work in these spaces as well as to work on them. Crucially too, as researchers it is important that we protect the spaces that we occupy from audit and surveillance that requires rigid adherence to a set of principles and protocols that have the potential to deny agency *with/in* these spaces. For researchers to be supported to examine the ethical dimensions of their work requires committees charged with this responsibility to become cognizant of contemporary research practices and to consider other ways they might work within their institutions. If we fail to question the performativity and performances of HRECs, will we, as qualitative researchers, be worked over rather than importantly working in them and *on them*?

References

Allen, A., K. Anderson, L. Bristol, Y. Downs, D. O'Neill, N. Watts, and Q. Wu. 2009. Resisting the unethical in formalised ethics: Perspectives and experiences. In *Power in the academy,* ed. J. Satterthwaite, H. Piper, and P. Sikes, 135–52. Staffordshire: Trentham.

Australian Government. 2007. *Australian code for the responsible conduct of research: Revised joint statement from the National Health and Medical Research Council, the Australian Research Council and Universities Australia.* http://www.nhmrc.gov.au/publications/synopses/e72syn.htm (accessed August 10, 2009).

Bauman, Z. 2000. On writing: On writing sociology. *Theory, Culture & Society* 17: 79–90.

Belmont Report. 1979. *The National Commission for the protection of human subjects of biomedical and behavioral research.* Report commissioned by The Department of Health, Education and Welfare, USA.

Bhabha, H. 1994. *The location of culture.* London: Routledge.

Chiapello, E., and N. Fairclough. 2002. Understanding the new management ideology: A transdisciplinary contribution from critical discourse analysis and new sociology of capitalism. *Discourse and Society* 13, no. 2: 185–208.

Collins, P. 1998. *Fighting words: Black women and the search for justice.* Minneapolis: University of Minnesota Press.

Cram, F. 2001. *Rangahau Māori: tona tika, tona pono* – The validity and integrity of Maori Research. In *Research ethics in Aotearoa,* ed. M. Tolich, 35–52. Auckland: Longman.

Fitzgerald, T. 2004. Powerful voices and powerful stories: Reflections on the challenges and dynamics of intercultural research. *Journal of Intercultural Studies* 25, no. 3: 233–45.

Grossman, M. 2004. Entangled subjects: Talk and text in collaborative indigenous Australian life-writing. PhD thesis, Monash University, Australia.

Halse, C., and A. Honey. 2005. Unravelling ethics: Illuminating the moral dilemmas of research ethics. *Signs: Journal of Women in Culture and Society* 30, no. 4: 2142–61.

Harding, S. 1987. *Feminism and methodology.* Bloomington: Indiana University Press.

Keenan, T. 1997. *Fables of responsibility: Aberrations and predicaments in ethics and politics.* Stanford: Stanford University Press.

Marker, M. 2003. Indigenous voice, community and epistemic violence: The ethnographer's 'Interests' and what 'Interests' the ethnographer. *Qualitative Studies in Education* 16, no. 3: 361–75.

Menzies, C. 2001. Reflections on research with, for and among indigenous peoples. *Canadian Journal of Native Education* 25, no. 1: 19–36.

Moreton-Robinson, A. 2000. *Talkin' up the White woman: Indigenous women and feminism.* Queensland: University of Queensland Press.

Ross, J. 2008. Why Australia needs a research ombudsman. *Campus Review* 11, no. 3: 8–9.

Smith, L. 1999. *Decolonizing methodologies: Research and indigenous peoples.* London: Zed Books.

White, J., and T. Hay. 2005. Passport to the profession: Standards based portfolios. In *Portfolios, performance and authenticity,* ed. T. Hay and J. Moss, 61–73. Frenchs Forest, NSW: Pearson.

Overstepping the mark: ethics procedures, risky research and education researchers

Catherine Lomas Scott[a] and Lariane Fonseca[b]

[a]*Teaching, Learning and Leadership Program, Australian Council for Educational Research, Camberwell, Victoria, Australia;* [b]*Swinburne Professional Learning, Swinburne University of Technology, Melbourne, Australia*

The authors reflect on the nature and experience of the process of ethics approval applied to educational research in Australia. Drawing on examples, dysfunctional aspects are identified, which impact most powerfully on particular individuals and groups. Possible explanations for the current situation are discussed, and an argument is made for a fundamental revision to a system which is unfit for the purpose.

Introduction

This contribution[1] focuses on problems encountered by both university staff and post-graduate students when attempting to conduct research in schools, and particularly when proposing research designed to explore sensitive issues. The damage incurred by individual researchers, the frustration of legitimate intentions of school principals and potential research funders, the inappropriate treatment of very young pupils, and the special vulnerability of postgraduate students arising from delay or interruption to their research, are all highlighted. Of central concern is the way in which the needs of educational researchers, university students, school teachers, managers and principals, as well as pupils, are being ill served by ethical review procedures and regulations, which are manifestly unfit for the purpose. Rather than being focused on the imperative to avoid unacceptable risk to research subjects, they actually treat both research subjects and researchers as potential risks in themselves. Instead of facilitating educational research to achieve good, they principally seek to avoid harm, and in so doing thwart the potential for research-based educational understanding and enhancement. The situation is, in part, the result of the way that in Australia all educational research is considered for ethical approval, along with all social science-related work, by committees responsible for 'human research'. These tend to be dominated by scientific and clinical awareness and assumptions, and include many colleagues who have little or no expertise or experience in social, scientific or educational research. This contributes to committee judgements inappropriate to educational research, and particularly to any which employ qualitative methods or 'risky' representational techniques. The work of these committees is administered by influential non-academic officers, and informal participant research by one of the authors into their work and approach is reported and discussed. Increasingly risk averse to social, political and institutional culture, these problems are magnified if research proposals engage with any of the sensitive issues present in relations between adults and children, teachers and pupils, as concern for the public profile of the university becomes a critical influence. While the changing political and policy contexts in which these developments have taken place are discussed, the emphasis is on the experience of educational researchers and the negative implications of current dysfunctional procedures for them, for postgraduate students, for teachers, for school principals, for pupils and for the educational mission itself.

'Getting through ethics' in Australia: tip-toeing through a minefield

Ethics review has been a part of Australian university life for over four decades. In a typical Australian university there are up to three ethics committees, respectively responsible for animal research, biomedical/bio-safety and human research. Proposals for educational research are assessed by the third of these. Australian human research ethics committees were originally established to oversee biomedical research with human participants, but this oversight was extended to social science, including educational research. As a consequence, the very real possibility of harm to people who participate in biomedical research was translated into the assumption of similar levels of risk for those who take part in educational or other social science-based research. In spite of the absence of evidence of even minor harm occurring to participants in research of this type, let alone widespread or significant harm or risk, a regime of oversight was instituted that is based on a presumption of guilt on the part of researchers. This has, over time, become increasingly complex, demanding, intrusive and difficult to satisfy (Scott 2003).

Inquiries to the national body that oversees Australian human research ethics, the National Health and Medical Research Council (NHMRC), have yielded no evidence of systematic attempts to evaluate the outcomes for participants, researchers or the university sector as a whole of the imposition of research ethics procedures, nor for the necessity of continually revising these in the direction of more stringency. The personal experiences of educational researchers, however, indicate that the research enterprise has been harmed by these assumptions and procedures.

A critical account of the activities and character of American Institutional Review Boards (IRBs) is offered by Fiske (2009). In Australian universities the emphasis on preventing harm rather than promoting good has made it increasingly difficult for a proposal to pass through the ethics process without being required to be amended in some way (Scott 2003). Further, certain classes of research and researchers are particularly at risk of having their research delayed or even prevented completely.

Risky techniques and risk-prone participants

A major factor underlying the ever-increasing complexity and intrusiveness of ethics procedures is the discovery of risks lurking in a lengthening list of research techniques. For example, in earlier regimes of ethics surveillance, it was considered that the actual completion of a questionnaire could be taken as proof of consent to be involved in the research; however, codes currently used in many universities demand that participants also complete informed consent instruments to signal their willingness to fill in the questionnaire. This added layer of complexity can be inconvenient, but attempts to use certain other 'high-risk' research techniques, especially with children, result in more than inconvenience.

'High-risk' procedures currently include videotaping or photographing participants, especially if these are children. Special measures are required of any researcher who films or photographs children, including the institution of security procedures to safeguard the images. This anxiety about photographing children reflects hysteria beyond the research context, in which making any images at all of children, in schools particularly, is now a minefield hedged around with dense thickets of required 'consent' (see Pope et al. this collection).

Another means by which ethics codes have become increasingly stringent and difficult to satisfy by educational researchers is the division of participants into categories, according to their supposed vulnerability. Children, the elderly, Indigenous people and those with disabilities are regarded as particularly at risk of exploitation by researchers. Consequently, anyone who proposes to conduct research with these groups faces added difficulty in gaining approval. The extra layers of 'protection' put between children and those who wish to conduct research in schools or classrooms has made life increasingly difficult for educational researchers.

Changing political and institutional responsibilities

Parallel to these developments in universities, the role played by the ethics committees of state departments of education in approving research has increased considerably. Anyone who wishes to conduct research in Australian government schools is required to have the research proposal assessed both by the relevant university ethics committee and by the department of education's committee(s) in the state(s) in which the research will be conducted. This discussion is based on the situation in the states with which the authors are most familiar.

Entry to state schools to conduct research has always been dependent on gaining the permission of the school principal, and this remains the case. Previously this was sufficient if the research was to be conducted in a single school, and only more extensive research in government schools required the approval of the education department's ethics committee. However, the reliance on principals' judgement concerning research proposed for their school has now been supplanted by the requirement that all research must be assessed by the state committee.

There is an unspoken factor underlying these changes: the dramatically increased amount of research conducted in or proposed for state schools in recent decades. The pressure on university teachers to conduct research has increased steadily, and the number of academics facing this pressure has also risen as a consequence of changes to post compulsory education in Australia since 1989 resulting from the 'Dawkins reforms'.[2] Prior to that date most teacher preparation was the responsibility of sub-university institutions, which had little or no tradition of conducting research, or in which research was positively discouraged in favour of teaching. With the advent of the Dawkins reforms, teachers' colleges and similar institutions were amalgamated with or upgraded to universities. Consequently, research became an accepted part of the work of teacher educators. It also became the expectation/requirement that academics in faculties of education would earn a doctorate. In addition, more and more postgraduate degrees were created and offered by the faculties of education in the upgraded institutions and these courses usually included a research project.

Valid concerns over the quality of research, plus the rapid increase in the number of researchers wishing to access schools, placed considerable pressure on the system that state education administrators sought to ameliorate, and 'raising the bar' for anyone seeking permission to enter schools to conduct research has been a part of this solution. A desire to protect schools, teachers and students from disruption and intrusion, from which they are rarely seen to benefit, is understandable. However, that this subtext now underlies ethics procedures gives the enterprise an element of 'bad faith', as the stated rationale differs from the actual purpose. It is also the case that state departments are increasingly concerned with the possibility that research will produce results that represent bad news for the public education system or some sub-section of it. Ethics procedures can be employed to prevent this possibility.

This change to the process of gaining approval for research is particularly significant for postgraduate students of education, including those studying to be school counsellors. As noted above, many master's degrees involved a research project. With some exceptions, particularly master's degrees in school counselling which are governed by the regulations of the psychology profession, universities progressively removed the project requirement, and arguably downgraded the rigour and value of the degree as a result. The difficulties placed in the way of student research by ethics committees played a part in this process.

The plight of postgraduates

Before the changes to state departmental ethics procedures, postgraduate students routinely reduced the probability of delay to commencing their studies by confining their research to one school. However, with the change of regulations, that was no longer possible. Many students, including school counsellor trainees, have only a single year to complete and write up their research. The requirement that research proposals must go through two sets of ethics procedures, with the student also needing to seek the school principal's approval, increases significantly the chances of a delay in commencement, and the resultant 'running over' of the project into the next year. For school counsellor interns, this coincides with commencement of full-time employment in their demanding new profession. Although a delay to finishing the project may be negotiated, commencing work as a full-time counsellor is mandatory and the combining of the two is difficult and taxing.

While it is certainly true that postgraduates, as trainee researchers, require guidance on their choice of topic, research design and adherence to ethical practice, in previous decades such guidance was regarded as the professional duty of their academic supervisor. In Australia, honours students and postgraduates were not required to submit their research to the ethics committee, and the latter were only required to have this assessed 'in house', by faculty-based committees. However, the general decline in trust in the propriety, trustworthiness and competence of professionals, academics included (Prickett and Erskine-Hill 2002), has licensed scrutiny of and intervention in the teacher–student relationship.

The consequences can be even more serious for international students. The number of fee-paying international research students studying in Australia has increased dramatically over the past 10 years. Frequently these students are in Australia for a limited period of time, supported by their governments and often their families. There is pressure to complete coursework, develop a research proposal, gain ethical clearance, undertake the research and write up within a limited period of time. Delays to ethics clearance can put great pressure on students to the extent that some have had to modify their research to something less involved, and potentially less valuable, in order to complete within time (see Hamid this collection). Some have had to complete the bulk of their research – with minimal supervision – after leaving Australia, because their visa has lapsed or financial support has come to an end. Similar problems can arise with domestic students bound by the regulations of various scholarships. In such cases, supervisors 'in the know' will steer their students towards simple replications and research designs in the hope that these will not attract too much attention.

Playing safe and the impoverishment of research

In the supervisory experience of the first author, the risk of being caught at the end of the second year of study with the research project not completed also helped to push counselling students towards the choice of 'safe' (usually instrument-driven) research, of the sort known to be easy to 'get through ethics'. These projects were usually replications with slight variations of projects already completed by students in previous cohorts, using well-known published instruments measuring attitudes or similar. Certainly students quickly learned that attempting any research of a clinical nature would be very difficult to have approved, as this would involve participants with a double dose of vulnerability, children with emotional or psychological difficulties. The consequence was that what could have been a valuable professional development experience tends to become a hurdle-jumping exercise, and the research conducted is stereotypical and impoverished.

Some students attempt to buck the trend, with sometimes negative consequences. One of the first author's counselling students attempted to conduct research of a clinical nature, which would have been of value and use to the school counselling profession. School counsellors are frequently required to work with students with emotional disorders, including anxiety problems. At the time of the incident reported here a brief intervention programme was in favour for use with children with anxiety problems. A previous student, now a practising counsellor, in the same guidance group had researched the effectiveness of this programme and found that participation resulted in improvement of symptoms, at least over the short-term. The first author's student wished to re-examine the children who had participated in the research to see if the improvement was maintained over the longer term. The university's ethics committee withheld approval for the research proposal on the grounds that it would be a 'violation of the privacy' of the participants in the original research. The student was unable to commence the research, with negative consequences for degree completion.

Of course, the privacy and confidentiality of research participants should be protected but the case demonstrates the extent to which ethics procedures are a blunt instrument, especially in the hands of committees with little understanding of the nuances of much social science, educational or clinical work. In a real sense, what the student proposed was an example of practitioner research, which observers have noted is exceptionally likely to encounter problems gaining ethics clearance (Pritchard 2002). The identity of persons suffering from disease and disorder must, by necessity, be shared among clinicians responsible for their care, and the same is true for school counsellors. This is not the same as carelessly or maliciously making public sensitive information about patients, pupils or clients. Certainly members of the guidance group were aware of the identity of children who were at risk of or suffering from problems, because of the nature of school counselling work and how it is organized. The human research ethics committee sought to mould reality to a 'research' template into which it did not fit, with unfortunate consequences. The case is also a fine example of the tendency for ethics committees to concentrate, overwhelmingly, on the prevention of harm rather than the doing of good.

Protecting children by silencing them

The consent of parents or guardians has always been necessary for certain types of educational research. However, increasingly, parents are asked to consent to children's participation even where children are to be 'just one of the crowd', rather than individually selected for participation. Recently the signed consent of children as young as four has become mandatory under codes adopted by at least some university ethics committees. State departmental ethics procedures do not require children to sign consent forms but the expectation is that the research, their participation in it and their right to withdraw from it will have been explained.

A major issue for educational researchers is that human research ethics committees frequently lack expertise in a wide range of techniques and methodologies utilized in educational research (see section 'Problems arising from committee membership and the "human factor"' on the mandatory composition of Australian university ethics committees). The minority of members who are academics are drawn from a wide range of specialisms; the committees frequently lack members with knowledge of child development and/or the day-to-day realities of schools. These issues can result in the prevention or major modification of research projects that involve schoolchildren.

The first author was peripherally involved in a case in which the 'stakeholders' most concerned with the issue being investigated (i.e. the children at the school where the research was to be conducted) were denied a voice by measures to 'protect' them from the harm supposedly posed by the research. The research was commissioned by the school itself and was concerned with student attainment. Planned techniques included analysis of achievement data, classroom observations and interviews with school personnel and students. The principal, as the instigator, had naturally consented to the research and parental consent was also to be sought. However, the ethics committee concerned (in this case chaired by a historian) determined that the children (aged five or six) were also to consent to being interviewed. Although they did not have to sign a consent form for the classroom observation component, they could withhold consent to participation. When queried over what was to be done if a child did this, the committee indicated that the child should be withdrawn from the classroom during observation periods. How the school or the researchers were to handle supervision of children opting out was not considered, and neither was the issue of what to do about learning experiences missed as a result of leaving the classroom. Further, the committee required that, as a condition of approval for the project, all children were to read and sign consent forms it drafted for the interview component. The forms were unsuitable in the extreme and required a reading age of approximately 16 to be read and understood. When it was pointed out that most children would not be able to read and understand the form's contents, and that many of the younger pupils could not read at all, the committee then indicated that the children should read the complex text, before signing their names.

It should be noted that the relevant state education department ethics committee neither requires nor approves of the signing of informed consent by school pupils. As a result of departmental policy, at this point the principal intervened and said that she would not permit her students to sign legal documents, given that they were minors and by law deemed not able to enter into contracts. The committee refused to change its ruling to allow interviews but the researchers were allowed to enter classrooms with the understanding that any student who wanted to leave during the observations could do so. None did. As a consequence of this process the research was conducted minus the input of the students, through the missing interview component.

Needless to say, in practice the research project was entirely unproblematic; the procedures proposed were of low risk and the potential harm to participants obscure in the extreme. Which harm was prevented by stopping the student interviews is difficult to imagine but the harm that was done by this decision was obvious: children were denied a say about their own schooling and the collection of useful and interesting data was prevented.

'Say anything to get them off our backs'

One paradoxical outcome of the current arrangements for ethics committee consideration of educational research in Australia is the extent to which these invite normally honourable people to contemplate disobeying the rules governing their professional behaviour in order that they be able to fulfil the research-related obligations of their roles. In the experience of the authors, many researchers in Australian universities respond to ethics committees by adopting a policy of doing or saying what is necessary to gain ethics approval. What then happens in the field can sometimes be another matter. The first author is not exempt from these strategic manoeuvres, as the following case illustrates.

Ethics committees in Australian universities exert their power over researchers by their ability to prevent access to research funding. University research offices both manage grants and other funding and house the ethics officers who provide administrative support to the ethics committees. Funds arriving at the research office alert the ethics committee to the probable submission of a research proposal for approval. Failure either to submit a proposal or to be given ethics approval means that the money will not be released.

In the example described here the money sent to the research office was not for research *per se*, but to fund a commissioned evaluation of the professional development offered by the regional office of a large education provider. The client specified that a number of strategically situated members of staff were to be included in the interviews scheduled. Polite insistence, by the academic responsible for the initiative, that the project was not research but programme evaluation and therefore did not require ethics approval was disregarded. Certainly the academic had some powerful evidence to support her case that what was proposed was not research. According to the American Code of Federal Regulations:

> *Research* means a systematic investigation, including research development, testing and evaluation, designed to develop or contribute to *generalizable knowledge* (emphasis added). (34 Code of Federal Regulations [CFR] 1991, 97.102[d])

A proposal was required however, which when submitted to the committee was rejected. The committee would not approve the project because of the intention that some personnel were to be interviewed regardless of their private feelings on the matter and this was taken to be a serious breach of the principle of informed consent. Also at issue was the inability to provide a detailed set of questions to be asked during the interviews.

The first author and her co-worker replied to the letter declining to give approval by pointing out that the project was not research, but evaluation. The funder and client had specified who was to be interviewed, and as an employer it had the right to require that its personnel participate in the evaluation. It was, in addition, impossible to specify, in advance, what questions would be asked, as these would emerge via an iterative process informed by issues that arose during the evaluation. However, the committee would not give ground and, anxious to match the reasonable expectations of the funder, the evaluation team determined and followed the line of least resistance. This required a fabricated informed consent instrument and some made up interview questions. The project was approved and the evaluation was conducted as it was originally designed.

Problems arising from committee membership and the 'human factor'

Particular problems created by the membership of specific ethics committees were touched-upon above, but the mandated composition of committees is a more widespread problem. The NHMRC has oversight of all human research conducted in Australia and its regulations dictate the composition of ethics committees. These specify that a majority of members should come from outside the research enterprise and that they should be representative of the unschooled community viewpoint or of non-research-related professional expertise (NHMRC 2007). The assumption is that they will thus be unbiased by any allegiance to the research enterprise in assessing the harmfulness or otherwise of proposed research. It seems more likely however, that they may be led by the supposed experts on the committee. Therein resides another set of problems, as the chairs of the ethics committees that assess education research proposals, and others from social science or humanities, can be drawn from outside these research traditions. Indeed, they may come from the non-human sciences and, as a result, gaining approval for even very innocuous educational research from a human research ethics committee can be unreasonably difficult.

The authors are not alone in discerning the difficulties arising from lack of appropriate expertise among committee members. Pritchard (2002, 7–8) has noted:

> IRBs should have the scientific expertise to judge the merits and weaknesses of whatever research projects they review. IRBs generally exist at institutions where the research experts on the IRB are a small minority of the research experts at the institution … when projects come to an IRB that are fundamentally different in nature from those it normally reviews, the IRB may simply lack the informed understanding necessary to judge a research project fairly.

Australian human ethics committees must, by mandate, also include at least one minister of religion or other person responsible for the pastoral care of a community, and at least one lawyer (NHMRC 2007). Members of these professions could potentially introduce problematic elements to the discussion of the safety of proposed research, but perhaps particularly lawyers, who have a professional mindset that includes discerning in any situation the worst case scenario in order to advise clients on avoiding or dealing with it. This professional 'risk aversion' could arguably push committees towards a focus on risk above all else (see Pritchard 2002, 8).

While working at a different Australian university from that referred to above, the first author was unable to commence the Australian phase of the Touchlines Project, investigating effects of heightened anxiety about physical contact between adults and children in schools and other care contexts, which in the UK was funded by the ESRC (see Piper and Stronach 2008).[3] This was the result of problems encountered with two ethics committees, including a university committee chaired by a mathematician (Scott 2008). The sensitivity of the issues to be investigated patently caused the university committee considerable concern, however, arguing the case for its importance was made doubly difficult by the necessity to negotiate with someone who had little knowledge of social science research methods and terminology. As a result the committee approved only the first questionnaire-based, and least problematic, phase of the research and withheld permission for the interview and observation phase.

In addition to difficulties at the university level, the state education department's ethics committee appeared in this case to be operating in 'gate-keeping mode', concerned to prevent research that might result in bad press for the department. In addition to the usual myriad trivial changes to wording of documents and to paperwork, the committee demanded that the name of the research project be changed and that, as well as speaking with teachers and students, the researcher also interview senior policy personnel and administrators. It is possible that the latter was in order that the teachers', presumably 'unreliable', testimony could be corrected 'for the record'; however, no reason was ever given for this demand. As the planned replication of the research in Australia was unfunded, and many months had passed without gaining approval from university or education department, the attempt to conduct the research was abandoned.

Beyond unfamiliarity with the relevant research traditions, other human factor issues seem to affect committee decisions. Membership of university committees is one way in which Australian academics can satisfy the 'service' component of their role specifications. However, as there are no knowledge or experience criteria required for membership of ethics committees, academic members can have little experience of research and may not be in a position to make appropriate judgements on the riskiness of research proposed. The principles that govern human behaviour in groups also predict that the committee member with the most extreme views is likely to become the leader, real or *de facto*, and thus push the committee towards more critical and vigilant attitudes to colleagues' research proposals (Baumeister 2005). All this has little to do with the ethical dimensions of research but it is nonetheless a real factor in how committees make their decisions.

Because the academic members of ethics committees tend to come and go, the person with the greatest corporate knowledge of the committee and its processes, and thus potentially the greatest influence, is usually the ethics officer, a general administrator charged with the support of the committee. These individuals often have no experience of the conduct of research. For two years the first author worked, on secondment, in research development at one Australian university and as a consequence became a participant observer among university ethics administrators, and was a part of their professional network, which is aided by electronic discussion groups, conferences and the like. To listen to and read their professional discussions was extremely instructive. Conversations had a distinct competitive edge: ethics officers were keen to paint the researchers at their own institutions as particularly 'bad' and requiring extraordinary surveillance and control efforts to 'keep them in line'. It appears inevitable that any such networks will have the effect of spreading aspects of practice and reputation between different universities and in the existing climate the likely result of this dissemination would be the further ratcheting up of the ethics requirements.

In Australian universities the status differential is normally in favour of academics and there seemed to be more than a little 'getting even' involved in some aspects of ethics officers' operations. The impulse to play up the status and importance of one's own work seemed to be little resisted by many and inevitably took the form of denigrating the stature, skills and knowledge of the researchers whose work was assessed by ethics committees. Those researchers at the receiving end of the results of these various 'human factor' and group dynamics issues may well find themselves accused of ignorance or lack of awareness if they query the committee's judgement. 'Answering back' can also lead to a reputation as being difficult at the very least, and can increase scrutiny of subsequent proposals.

'Non-standard' forms of scholarship

There is evidence that committees find it particularly difficult to judge the worth of research proposals that draw on less traditional research methods (Lincoln 2004). We have noted the tendency for ethics committees to attempt to force the intricacies of real world research into a rigid template, which it often does not fit. It can become even more complex when life itself, in the case of practitioner research (Pritchard 2002), must be accommodated to the particular and unrealistic universe of the ethics committee.

The first author witnessed a conspicuous example when senior educators, mainly school and college principals, enrolled on a doctorate in education, attempted to use their own practice as the basis for scholarly inquiry. The obvious truth that the conduct of daily professional life failed to meet the artificial demands of informed consent, and other ethical strictures, resulted in delays to the commencement of the research. For example, talking to staff in the course of career planning and performance appraisal for research purposes was deemed problematic by the committee. The ethics committee wanted to see in advance all the questions to be put to staff – an impossibility – and for full informed consent procedures to be implemented. The principals involved said that participation in professional development discussions was not voluntary but a mandated part of teachers' professional activities. Further, the focus of the research was the principals' own knowledge, skills and competence: what they really did know of their staff's needs and how effectively they were meeting them. Eventually the committee backed down. The experience demonstrated that what passes without comment in day-to-day life becomes highly problematic, and necessitates outside surveillance and control, when it is labelled 'research'.[4]

In a climate of risk avoidance, in which it is expected that there will be issues with any proposal that comes before the committee, there can be the tendency to trawl through each, looking for the weak spot or the risky procedure. Demands for changes that ensue, made in ignorance of the technicalities of the methods proposed, can be impossible to accommodate, leading to delay or derailing of the project. The second author's experience of gaining approval for her PhD research is an instructive example, and some initial context setting will be useful.

As already noted, anxiety about image-making is now ubiquitous, so that even photographing or videoing adults or the use of ancient family snaps has become an act that requires the explicit approval of all concerned, well beyond contexts that could be defined as 'research'. This seeming paranoia exists in a situation in which security cameras abound, and the innocent activities of citizens are routinely filmed without their consent. The Internet, mobile phones and other electronic devices provide endless opportunities for people to produce and propagate images with no regard for consent, and there is little apparent concern among those who participate in this common and proliferating pastime. The draconian control over the production and use of images in educational settings and during educational research seems strange, indeed, in this context (see Pope et al. this collection).

The university concerned has a history of requiring that an extraordinary range of materials be submitted to the ethics committee for approval, including quite routine work of consulting with students for feedback and needs analysis purposes (in case this should ever lead to publication of the outcomes). As an example, the body in the university charged with overseeing the improvement of teaching and learning produces reports of its activities and shares these widely. As a result, under the university's very wide definition of 'research', a great deal of the work performed by this unit is subject to ethics approval. The distorting effects of trimming and shaping proposals to 'get them through ethics' seem not to come into consideration.

Given that the university is 'post-1989', that is an upgraded poly-technical style institution with a weak history of research but a strong desire to increase its research profile, sheer inexperience and lack of understanding may explain the excesses committed. To lapse into thorough-going speculation, it may even be that a conspicuous ethics research apparatus may be seen as advertising the institution's identity as 'research active'. Perhaps simply counting the number of proposals heard may represent a very crude way of enhancing perceptions of its 'research profile'. Viewed this way, the demands of this particular committee are perhaps an example of the ways in which oversight and audit come to shape, not to say distort, what they are meant merely to supervise.

The most salient aspect of the second author's doctoral research is that it has no research participants as normally understood and thus fails to meet the American Federal government's definition for research. However, because of its autobiographical nature, it does inevitably implicate others. Issues raised by this aspect of (auto)biographical work have resulted in considerable debate about its ethical dimensions. However, the troubles described below did not arise because of the relevant committee's awareness of this debate but because of the widespread anxiety about the use of images or depictions of people and the committee's misinterpretation of state privacy legislation.

The work is an exploration of the development of identity in the context of the migration experience of the author. It consists of a number of illustrative artefacts, composed of text and pictures, with an exegesis. In its initial form the project was also to include interviews, and the original proposal was granted ethics clearance. The decision was made to omit the interviews, meaning that there were no longer any participants and, in theory, that the research was no longer subject to ethics processes. The committee was informed of the change of methods and its involvement should have stopped at that point. However, the committee withdrew its original approval and, under the requirement that 'depictions' of persons be subject to approval, ethics advisors demanded that the consent of the persons in all photographs and images used in the artefacts be obtained.[5]

This demand was not included in the original clearance given to the project[6] and was very difficult to satisfy, as contact had been lost many years before with many of the people depicted, and/or they lived dispersed over a number of countries separated by long distances. Leaving out key persons because they could not be contacted to approve the use of photographs would considerably compromise the integrity of the scholarship. At one stage of the negotiation process with the committee it was even suggested that faces of the people in the photographs should be 'smudged' so as to render them unidentifiable – ironic, given the thesis's focus on identity. It is also difficult to see what probable harm would result from the inclusion of very old photographs in any case, unless it is potential harm to the university via a law suit by some individual disgruntled at his or her image appearing in the thesis, a highly improbable outcome in any case. The project remains 'unapproved' at the time of writing.

Conclusion

In this contribution we have faithfully reported instances we have experienced or witnessed. The question that we often asked of those committees that found fault with our research proposals, and those of our students, may have also occurred to some readers: what does this have to do with protecting the interests of research participants? In truth the answer is that human research ethics governance in Australian universities has little to do with protecting participants at all.

We have explored a variety of 'human' and group dynamics factors that we have speculated may have contributed to the constantly increasing power of ethics committees and their movement towards ever more extreme regimes of regulation, all in the context of a total lack of evidence of harm or even credible threat of harm to participants. It is undoubtedly true that university administrations could have reined in their ethics committees and prevented them from becoming the enemies of research and researchers. That they did not do so is instructive. There is nothing rational about the process we have described. It is arguably a singular type of institutional psychiatric symptom, a particular manifestation of deep distress in the Australian university system.

The answer to the puzzle lies in understanding the socio-political context in which Australian universities attempt to do their work. The first author commenced her university career before the Dawkins reforms of the late 1980s and can thus remember the time when ethics procedures were a mild and undemanding affair, easily dealt with. The situation changed with the Dawkins reforms; the turmoil they unleashed in the university system was considerable and the fallout continues to the present day. Soon after their enactment, Australia elected a conservative government that stayed in power for the next 11 years. Like most conservative administrations the government of Prime Minister John Howard was no particular friend of education (Prickett and Erskine-Hill 2002). The university sector, still struggling to come to terms with the massive restructure visited on it by the Dawkins reforms, found itself simultaneously stripped of funding, resources and autonomy, and subject to a constantly escalating set of demands and expectations, including an onerous and intrusive regime of surveillance and control. This last point may sound familiar.

One aspect of the increasing expectations placed on universities and their staff has been that they increase their research activity. For the Federal government this was in order to maintain Australia's international 'competitiveness'; for individual universities it was to maintain or achieve an edge in the competition with the others. Rumours of a return to the previous 'binary divide', with some institutions returned to lower 'teach only' status, maintained an atmosphere of high tension as each university administration attempted to motivate or goad its staff into sufficient research activity to avoid (hypothetical) relegation.

For 'post-1989' universities the situation was particularly difficult because they started their life with few or no research-active staff and were faced with developing existing staff members' research expertise or hiring new staff with appropriate experience; the latter is very problematic for cash-strapped institutions with little to offer a 'high-flyer'. As funding for research was ratcheted down, the competition to obtain necessary support also became increasingly fierce and new universities found it difficult to compete with established institutions for the funds that would allow them to begin to establish a research profile. In a sense it is no wonder that research ethics became the focus of such tension and conflict and it has been our observation, noted above, that newer universities seem to have regimes of ethics clearance that are even more contentious and convoluted. Hard-pressed university administrations now occupied a landscape of continual threat in a hostile environment. It is not fanciful to see their hostile and punitive stance towards their own staff and students as the reflection of developments in the wider environment. Examination of the behaviour of ethics committees reveals a constant scanning of the environment for risk of harm – not to research participants but to the university itself.

Each change of legislation brings the possibility that someone somewhere will use this against the university. Researchers are in a sense the institution's weak link both because the status of the university rides on their efforts and because they have transactions with people from the 'outside', that is, the various participants in research. These outsiders pose a risk to the university because they may decide that their ephemeral association with it has harmed them in some way and they might resort to the law as a consequence. Participating in the conversations of ethics officers revealed that they spoke of participants not as *being at risk* but as *posing a risk* – to the university. Those involved in research governance expend a great deal of time and energy searching for more and more loopholes through which danger may infiltrate the university and then seeking to plug these by tighter and tighter restrictions on research. Like any psychiatric manifestation of anxiety however, the rituals and obsessions bring no relief but serve to remind all concerned of their vulnerability.

If this analysis is correct, the solution to continual interference with educational research by university ethics committees does not lie in at last being able to make the personnel concerned understand that the harm they do is monumental in comparison to that which they may prevent. Rather it lies in the hope that Australian universities will be allowed to emerge from the dark period they have endured for two-and-a-half decades, into an era of relative stability. Freed of toxic environmental influences, some sort of balance will hopefully return to university processes for assessing the value and potential, as well as the risks, of research into educational issues and contexts proposed by their staff and students.

Notes

1. Here we explore and reflect upon personal experiences of educational research interrupted or prevented by processes of ethical approval currently operative in Australian universities. The authors write from the vantage point of working in seven universities and more than two decades of first hand, in-depth experience of educational research in Australia and this experience is the basis for the strength of the claims we make. Confidentiality and a

commitment to ethical practice compel us to not 'name names' nor identify all our sources but we write, nonetheless, from a position of integrity.

2. The Dawkins reforms were named after the Federal Minister for Education, John Dawkins, who introduced them in the late 1980s. Under these reforms sub-university institutions that offered programmes of tertiary education, including teachers' colleges, were either upgraded to university status or amalgamated with existing universities. Similar reforms in the UK saw polytechnics become universities in 1992.
3. Piper, H., I. Stronach, and M. MacLure. 2006. Touchlines: The problematics of touching between children and professionals. *ESRC funded project RES-000-22-0815*.
4. Feedback from the relevant state department of education was that the resulting report was one of the most useful they had received and findings of the research have been included in professional development training for aspiring principals.
5. The committee concerned justified its stance by reference to state privacy legislation. However, consultations with the relevant government authority revealed that the legislation did not apply in the circumstances and should not have been cited to support the committee's decision.
6. This in itself is an illustrative example of how demands for compliance and conditions for approval are continually ramped up, even within the life of a single project.

References

34 Code of Federal Regulations. 1991. Part 97 Federal policy for the protection of human subjects. *Federal Register* 56, no. 117: 28003–32.

Baumeister, R. 2005. *The cultural animal: Human nature, meaning and social life.* New York: Oxford University Press.

Fiske, S. 2009. Institutional review boards: From bane to benefit. *Perspectives on Psychological Science* 30, no. 1: 30–1.

Hamid, M.O. 2010. Fieldwork for language education research in rural Bangladesh: ethical issue and dilemmas. *International Journal of Research & Method in Education* 33, no. 3: 259–271.

Lincoln, Y.S. 2004. Qualitative research and institutional review boards. *Qualitative Inquiry* 10, no. 2: 219–34.

National Health and Medical Research Council. 2007. *Overview of Human Research Ethics Committees (HRECs).* http://www.nhmrc.gov.au/health_ethics/hrecs/overview.htm. (accessed 4 March 2009)

Piper, H., and I. Stronach, eds. 2008. *Don't Touch! The educational story of a panic.* London/New York: Routledge.

Pope, C.C., R. De Luca, and M. Tolich. 2010. How an exchange of perspectives led to tentative ethical guidelines for visual ethnography. *International Journal of Research & Method in Education* 33, no. 3: 301–315.

Prickett, S., and P. Erskine-Hill. 2002. *Education! education! education! Managerial ethics and the law of unintended consequences.* Thorverton, UK: Imprint Academic.

Pritchard, I.A. 2002. Travellers and trolls: Practitioner research and institutional review boards. *Educational Researcher* 31, no. 3: 3–13.

Scott, C. 2008. Relationships: Ethics committees and research. In *Don't Touch! The educational story of a panic,* ed. H. Piper and I. Stronach, 12–22. London/New York: Routledge.

Scott, C.L. 2003. Ethics and knowledge in the contemporary university. *Critical Reviews in International Social and Political Philosophy* 6, no. 4: 93–107.

How an exchange of perspectives led to tentative ethical guidelines for visual ethnography

Clive C. Pope[a], Rosemary De Luca[b] and Martin Tolich[c]

[a]*Department of Sport & Leisure Studies, University of Waikato, Box 3105, Hamilton 3140, New Zealand;* [b]*Department of Professional Studies, University of Waikato, Box 3105, Hamilton 3140, New Zealand;* [c]*Department of Anthropology, Gender & Sociology, University of Otago, Box 56, Dunedin 9054, New Zealand*

Qualitative research, especially visual ethnography, is an iterative not a linear process, replete with good intentions, false starts, mistaken assumptions, miscommunication and a continually revised statement of the problem. That the camera freezes everything and everyone in the frame only complicates ethical considerations. This work, jointly authored by the researcher, the Research Ethics Committee (REC) chair and an informed outsider, walks the reader through the ethical challenges the researcher experienced seeking REC approval to conduct a visual ethnography of a secondary school's rowing event. Eventually, the researcher found the challenges and ambiguities of informed consent indicative of the current issues facing many researchers working with the visual medium. The account fleshes out a procedural ethics and ethics in practice dichotomy and ends with the researcher and REC chair retrospectively contemplating the iterative ethics of visual ethnography. We conclude our conversation by proposing five tentative guidelines for visual ethnography researchers and their research ethics committees.

Backdrop

The first author of this account took over 500 photographs in a 10-day visual ethnographic case study of a secondary school's rowing regatta. One photograph (see Figure 1) is particularly helpful in teasing out fundamental ethical issues facing visual ethnographers. Thus, we can assume both that these medal winners were photographed by persons in the crowd and that their photo appeared in the regional daily newspaper. Few would have ethical issues with this action. However, had the author, a university researcher, snapped the winners on the dais for research purposes, his Research Ethics Committee (REC) would require him to get their consent to photograph and then publish. Why are institutionally based researchers constrained in this way? In this instance, the researcher did not take a photo directly but took a photo of a video image in a public place. The medalists are clearly recognizable. Should the researcher now be obliged to obtain the medalists' permission (and maybe the TV company's) before using the photograph?

With regard to seeking and gaining consent, taking photographs can produce an ethical quandary for visual ethnographers. In the second part of this paper, we address some of these consent issues. Firstly though, we briefly situate the emergence of visual research, having taken note of a literature laden with ethical challenges. We end Part 1 by documenting the first author's ethics review application before moving on to consider issues and concerns around the researcher taking photos and videos in public space.[1]

Introduction

To understand the experiences students seek and gain through sport, the researcher conducted an ethnography of the largest secondary school sporting event that occurs in New Zealand. The regatta took place over 10 days leaving insufficient time for a sole researcher to observe, record and code field notes *in situ*. Opting for a visual ethnography not only enabled documentation of the wider culture of rowing in detail but also made it possible to revisit what had been captured through the lens post event.

Specifically, a visual ethnography offered a chance to embrace new technologies and broaden opportunities to investigate human experience. However, such an exercise was not unproblematic.

The competition that occurred in the rowing lanes was matched by the researcher's endeavour to gain approval for the project from his institution's REC.[2] The REC chair is the second author. Although the study was located within the open spaces of a public sports venue, it was still subject to the ethics conventions of the REC. Why is it that ethical approval appears to be readily granted for qualitative research methodologies using participant observation, semi-structured interviews and document analysis but when a camera or video camera is proposed as a research tool the scrutiny intensifies? Why and how the camera reconfigures ethical considerations has been explored below.

The uptake of visual methods within education has exposed several research ethics problems (Pink 2007; Prosser 1992, 2000) compounded by an acknowledged lack of convention associated with visual ethics. The rising popularity of images as a research method highlights the need to address the emerging state of image ethics in ethnographic research. This position endorses Prosser's advocacy for an agreed understanding of the contribution of images as evidence to research and perhaps more importantly of, 'what constitutes a framework for proper ethical use of photography in school' (Prosser 1992, 410). Any barriers and conservatism within educational research must be overcome if the potential of images in educational research is to be realized (Allen 2009; Prosser 2007).

For progress in qualitative research ethics to be made, internal and external problems must be drawn from the periphery of the research conversation to its epicentre. And a vital part of this conversation must be image ethics. The distinctive ethical issues created by visual research must be recognized and addressed if Prosser's (2000) moral maze is to be negotiated and the development of ethical guidelines for visually oriented research is a priority. Researchers and ethics committees face a weighty and pressing challenge. The conversation could start with the following argument:

> For visual social science to develop, professional rules and norms concerning ethics must acknowledge the rights of photographers/researchers to photograph in public and to present identifiable subjects, but in the context of ethical considerations that consider photographers/researchers as connected by *webs of obligation and moral regard.* [emphasis added] (Harper 2005, 760)

The salience of this quotation, the balance between multiple rights and context, frames our writing. It documents the encounters and dilemmas of an ethical nature faced by the researcher leading up to and during this visual ethnography and some of the second author's (REC chair's) responses to it. The third author, from another university, brings a 15-year experience of serving on ethics committees and writing about qualitative research ethics to review both the application and the REC's responses to it. His contribution finds flaws in both the initial ethics application and the rigidity of the procedural ethics process, and the mandatory predisposition toward informed consent. Yet he also finds great flexibility in the ethics in practice. The article demonstrates how rigid ethical prescriptions can yield in the field to both the researcher's and the REC's satisfaction.

Part 1: Ethical approval and ambiguity

Before discussing the visual ethics of this research, it is important to note that the researcher does acknowledge that the ethics application could have been packaged better. The format of the original application did not sufficiently distinguish the five data collection methods. Seeking ethical approval for all five techniques – observation, photovoice, semi-structured interviews and video and still image photography – at once failed to address the nuances of the ethics of each technique and made comprehension by the REC difficult. Subsequent miscommunication was unavoidable and was only unravelled during the initial discussion around writing this account.

What follows is part of the original application. On reflection a simple demarcation in each sub-section for each technique would have simplified the application, allowing the ethics committee to respond to each technique's ethical considerations in turn. Note that the selected section of the application below discusses only one technique, photovoice. It should have been written in five sub-parts outlining access to participants and informed consent procedures for all sub-parts:

> Access to participants will be sought through [New Zealand Secondary Schools Rowing Association] NZSSRA and the respective secondary schools. Each school will be asked to invite one coach and three students for interviews and a further four students as photovoice contributors. Students could be both interviewees and photovoice contributors. These volunteers will be purposefully sampled to gain a gender and experience balance. These individuals will then be contacted individually to arrange face to face interview times and locations. Interviews will be conducted at the respective schools, the school training site or at Lake Karapiro. Interviews conducted at the latter site will take place in a separate tent to avoid distraction and external noise.
>
> … an information sheet will be provided to the participants specifying the purpose of the research investigation, the uses and who will have access to this data, as well as outlining the expectations of the participants in the study in an Appendix. Similarly, an informed consent form will be administered to the participants, and parent/caregiver, if necessary. This will explain the individual's rights during the study, such as access to information and their right to terminate their involvement at any stage. These consent forms will need to be signed and returned to the researcher before the participant can be admitted into the project. Examples of these forms have been included in Appendices.

This application excerpt does not adequately tease apart the five separate techniques let alone address each method's unique ethical issues sufficiently for an ethics committee to provide a clear decision. To an outsider, such as the third author, miscommunication between the researcher and ethics committee was inevitable. Yet in the researcher's defence, his full ethics application did address the ethical issues of each of the five techniques, although these were dispersed throughout the application. For example, in the section *Procedure for recruiting participants and obtaining informed consent*, the three separate phases of the research project are outlined. Phase 1 and Phase 3 involve semi-structured interviews both before and after the event with students and coaches in various schools. Phase 2 involving visual media is less straightforward, focusing on the ethical issues raised by both videotaping public space, and co-opting adolescents to participate in photovoice. Here is an excerpt from the original application. Note that the two parts of Phase 2 are unfortunately clumped together as though they were one phase, when the sub parts, photovoice and videotaping/photographing, should have been dealt with separately throughout the application:

> Phase 2 will occur on-site.
>
> Two days prior to the Maadi Cup week of competition I will establish myself at Lake Karapiro. I will live amongst the competitors based in a camper (a camp site has been booked for this purpose). Throughout the Maadi meet I will record this event using digital cameras, video camera and Dictaphones. With appropriate permission (obtained through the School of Education ethics process) I will collect images and sounds of the weeks' events. These will be downloaded and securely stored for analysis. Although there is debate regarding the ethics of visual research this medium is still in its infancy. As Prosser has recently stated 'the ethics of visual research … [is] located somewhere near the centre of a complex moral maze.' (Prosser, 2000, p. 132). Moreover, to date there is little consensus within the Social Sciences about what should be the appropriate guidelines and codes of practice for this burgeoning medium. Perhaps the most important consideration for researchers is an acknowledgement of the potential ethical dilemmas visual research reveals and also revisit the underpinning tenet that researchers are ethically obligated to their subjects. Like many educational institutions venues such as Lake Karapiro (where this event is being held) is neither a public nor a private place, thereby exacerbating the legal position even more.
>
> Because part of this project endeavours to gain an insight to how youth experience this event I will seek the assistance of 10–12 young people to collect images of the week that will be taken on either cell-phone cameras or with disposable Kodak cameras. Each participant will be offered a $20 phone card to cover costs. Students will be asked to interpret their image selections post event through both electronic and/or face-to-face means. The adoption of photovoice provides another medium through which young people can communicate their interests and ideas using a tool that has become integral to their lifestyles. The former will occur through email while the latter will occur through interviews. Shortly after the Maadi Cup regatta follow-up interviews will be conducted with the same respondents as the pre-event participants.

Until recently the first author believed the ethical sticking point in his application was his videotaping of the rowing event. It was not, although the REC did place restrictions around informed consent. The committee held the researcher in high esteem and assumed he would act ethically. The REC's main concern was with the photovoice technique: giving cameras to untrained teenagers was deemed high risk. The researcher, until the debrief in preparation to write this article, assumed the photovoice issues had been clarified. They had not. The second author, the REC chair, had fewer problems with the videotaping/photographing data collection than with consent issues involved in co-opting school pupils to take photographs of their friends. Thus, issues of informed consent in Phase 2 (photovoice and photographing) became the focus of the REC's response. In the next section, the researcher provides a brief account of one of his five research techniques, still photography.

An ethical constraint

After an extended period of negotiation between the researcher and the REC chair, approval was eventually given. However, this formal ethics review process did raise several ethical issues, notably the informed consent requirements to photograph and videotape. Some of these could be addressed, some were ameliorated on site and some were actually compounded in the field by the presence of both commercial photographers and a television company.

In addition to gaining approval from the School Rowing Association and the principals of four selected secondary schools, the REC stipulated the author place notices around the regatta venue advertising the intention of the research project. This notification was reinforced by periodic announcements over the public address system during the week's competition detailing the purpose of the research and who was conducting it.

Once on-site, the researcher proceeded to spend the week observing, interviewing, photographing and video recording the life and times of the people and events associated with this sporting spectacle. Days would commence at 5.30 am as competitors and support staff embarked on their highly planned and structured routines. Over 2000 students, plus parents, coaches, administrators and officials as well as millions of dollars of equipment filled the grounds around the lake every day. The highly dynamic and constantly changing landscape had to be both rapidly and appropriately documented. However, the procedural ethics had influenced what thinking and decision-making took place before the shutter was clicked.

As the lens was adjusted and the researcher's first finger slid onto the elevated button the words of the ethics committee's approval letter – 'if the photographs are to be used in research publications then you must ensure that informed consent is gained and recorded from those people whose photos have been used' – acted as the equivalent of the safety catch before the button was depressed. Should the spontaneity of the photo be sacrificed to gain prior verbal or written approval to photograph? If the photo were taken after approval was gained, would it be a realistic representation? If a competitor(s) is photographed but lost in the crowd by the time the photographer reaches his or her position should the photo then be deleted? Could that photo be retained if it were deemed not harmful or deemed that the event organizers had approved permission in *loco parentis*? If competitors cannot be reached (they may be on the lake competing or engaged in a team meeting) does retaining that image amount to misappropriation? Does showing the face of defeat on an athlete amount to harm? Equally, can showing success lead to harm?

The third author, an outsider to this project, is intrigued by the extent of the informed consent requirements. On one hand, individual consent was required for each photograph, but on the other hand, public announcements disclosing the presence of the researcher provided secondary coverage. For the researcher, perhaps the most difficult quandary associated with informed consent was the threshold for individual versus passive consent when more than one person was in the photograph. There were numerous team, group or crowd shots taken. Figure 2 shows an example of a crowd photo. Is it realistic to gain consent from every recognizable face in this frame? If a crowd shot reveals 65 people who can be recognized then should all 65 sign informed consent forms? If 65 is unrealistic then at what number or criterion does it become realistic to get consent? This issue is further exacerbated by the number of faces that can be identified in one pan of a video camera. The rapid advancement of technology has meant that high quality pixilation and resolution can now be achieved by digital photography for a modest cost. The detail and depth of field of photos have been considerably enhanced making it possible to identify faces in what used to be a quite fuzzy or blurred product.

Wrestling with ethical issues such as anonymity was compounded by the public nature of the research context. The researcher's multiple strategies to protect participants were increasingly aggravated by the very public expressions of display that popped up in numerous guises. This entire event was televised throughout New Zealand on one of the subscriber sports channels, offering their production crews the chance to practice for the 2010 world championships to be held at this venue. In addition to the live coverage to the homes around the country, a large screen was part of the local landscape for all finals days (see Figure 1). There was also a professional photography company present, taking and selling images on-site and via the Internet. These very public recordings, juxtaposed with the researcher's nomadic wandering and photographing, were unrestrained by the same conventions he had been asked to observe. There was a quite obvious blurring of what is public and what is private, as represented in Figure 1. The researcher manoeuvring around to avoid face shots (see Figures 5 and 6) while competitors were openly posing for photos on cell phones created an ironic public/academic binary for visual ethnography.

Part 2: Framing the ethics

Part 2 features five selected photographs taken from the researcher's visual ethnography. We reiterate that space has limited our attention only to photos taken by

Figure 1. The TV monitor.

the researcher. The three authors first discuss the ethical issues involved in each photograph before offering a reflective summary of all six photographs. Following this the researcher and the REC chair reflect, retrospectively, on what they individually learned about ethics from their part in this visual ethnography. Part 2 ends by presenting tentative guidelines for visual ethnography.

Researcher

After several days of working within the given ethics conventions, I became somewhat frustrated at the double standard of overt projection of competitors from the resident sport channel broadcasting these images at the lake and throughout the country.

REC chair

Researcher and journalists have clearly defined roles, and codes of ethics apply respectively. Researcher judgement and ethical awareness are critical, part of a connection to 'webs of obligation and moral regard' (Harper 2005, 760) as referred above. There does seem to be a higher level of tolerance and more acceptable exercise of licence for journalists than research codes allow. Figure 1 here is a situation for the researcher to exercise his judgement.

Third author

The researcher did not take a photo directly but took a photo of a video image in a public place. The medallists are clearly recognizable but these people are on public display, inviting a photograph. Consent is not required.

Figure 2. The event.

Researcher

This shot portrays the colour, magnitude and festival associated with this event. As the week progressed the crowds were built incrementally. I wanted to project the wider public interest and support for this event even though rowing is regarded as a minor sport in New Zealand. (Note the large video monitor in the background.) Because this frame included so many people and so much detail, consent was aligned to the event organizers' approval. In my mind taking this photo would not create harm.

REC chair

There is the question of consent, both to photograph in the first place and then to publish. Information about the project was available to all present at the regatta. Schools, in particular, had been alerted. Whilst contributing significantly to the ethnographic intent, the image seems innocuous from an ethical perspective. People in the foreground are probably recognizable, but they are adults and do not appear to object to the camera's presence. My advice is to go ahead and use the photograph without explicit consent.

Third author

This is a crowd scene and not of anyone in particular. The American Sociological Association guidelines on gaining informed consent in public places can be taken to support taking pictures like this, of public places. It was not necessary to warn the crowd in advance before taking this type of photo. I note that the REC chair, above,

Figure 3. Photos of competitors for purchase on-site or on the Internet.

has deemed the photograph innocuous. I am left wondering if more discretion or more nuanced guidelines can be given to researchers beyond mandatory informed consent.

Researcher

Another ironic situation. Event organizers did not permit me to photograph on the water but the commercial photography company was allowed. Working under these restrictions acted like sandpaper against the freedom and commercial agenda of the on-site photography company. I could not help but reflect on the power of business and media. Taking this photo occurred as I considered there to be minimal, if any, risk.

REC chair

The image is innocuous from a research ethics perspective, a situation for the researcher to exercise his own judgement.

Third author

The three people pictured are incidental to the photo. No consent is necessary, as no harm could arise. The irony is palpable vis-à-vis ethics governing institutional and commercial ethics. Again, procedural ethics consent requirement fades when exposed by the banality of everyday life.

Researcher

While I had permission from the school's staff to photograph their people, I did not have permission from two male students depicted in the background. The other two factors were that the group of 10 young women were lounging about – this was down time, chilling out, pre- or post-race – but not really doing anything substantive yet it was an important part of the day for all competitors. The more delicate issue for me was the two female students intertwining their legs in the foreground. The image could have projected an impression of intimacy, potentially harming the two girls.[3] I just felt uneasy about this.

Figure 4. The photograph was deleted by the researcher. It showed a group of 10 girls lounging under a tent. In the background are two boys walking past the tent.

REC chair

I noticed the position of the legs but did not read anything into it. However, the researcher's different response illustrates researcher sensitivity and judgement at work.

Third author

This deletion demonstrates researchers' ethics in practice: how consent to photograph participants is mediated by the researcher's ethical considerations at the point of reproduction, not necessarily at the point of data collection.

Researcher

While there were numerous shots taken celebrating success at this regatta there were also times of disappointment. That is the nature of sport. This was an example of how friends or team mates are a vital part of dealing with times of distress. The image captured the spontaneity of support that often occurs in sporting contexts. I did not ask the students for their consent to take this image. I felt that intruding during this delicate time was more harmful than using the image for future publication without their consent. I knew I had the permission of the school and the event organizers.

REC chair

Here, I question the intimacy of the moment being caught on camera and then subsequently made public, and also the intrusion on the part of the researcher who must have stood very close to the pair although they were almost certainly unaware. I think,

Figure 5. Positioned for anonymity?

on balance, I would not use this image without consent. I would argue on the basis of privacy. However, in defence of publication it could be argued that this scene was probably replicated hundreds of times during the course of the regatta. The young woman facing the camera is probably not identifiable, and her facial features could be blurred anyway to safeguard against identification.

Third author

I do not know the background for this photograph. The photo may capture an informal but intimate counselling session, the person facing the camera seems upset; face and cap are down. I assume the person let someone down or lost a boy/girlfriend.

Researcher

This shot captures the post-event cocktail of exhaustion, resolution and emotional release. It reflects how public such reactions can end up being, while at the same time they can be quite isolating and private. This photo differs from Figure 5 as I had more time to frame the shot and select a moment when faces were obscured. Also their physical state of exhaustion would be considerably less problematic than the focus of Figure 5 on an emotional state.

REC chair

No one is identifiable here, and this is a typical situation. I have no problem with the image being published, or the photograph being taken in the first place. It is different

Figure 6. Does post-race despair require consent?

from the image in Figure 5, essentially by the others around these young women seeming to have accepted a level of openness that is absent from Figure 5. This image also lacks the palpability the other one evokes.

Third author

As with Figure 5, in Figure 6 context overrides consent. Informed consent is not the sole issue here, as internal confidentiality (Tolich 2004) is a problem. The person's identity is unclear and gives external confidentiality, but if the photograph was published everyone in the person's school will know who the person is. The main ethical issue is contextual in terms of its potential harm. This photo captures exhaustion whereas the other photograph captured emotion. Given this ambiguity, maybe consent is required for Figure 5 but not for Figure 6.

The three authors' reviews

Third author's summary

These photographs elaborate Guillemin and Gillam's (2004) procedural ethics and ethics in practice dualism. Taking the photograph is one important task, but this activity is balanced within the context in which it is presented. Figures 1 (monitor), 2 (the crowd) and 3 (commercial photography booth) do not need consent, nor do they need prior announcement. Yet having made this distinction a more nuanced distinction must be made between what is public and private. Is a photograph of all a school's entire rowing team a crowd? The issue of numbers of people in a single photograph needs further thought but the emerging principle discovered in this discussion is that not all photographs taken in public space require mandatory consent. The REC's requirement that the researcher repeatedly announce his presence over the public address system falls more into research governance or risk management frame, at best passive consent rather than considered ethical practice. For example, by what process would a member of the public opt out from the first author's research?

Figures 5 and 6 highlight the importance of context. Even though the persons are not identifiable, their school friends may read the article and make out either of them and harm may ensue. Figures 5 and 6 are instructive to the visual ethics debate. When ethical issues are not limited to informed consent more robust ethical considerations develop.

Figure 3 (commercial photographs) demonstrates the limits placed on academics by their institutions, yet these six photographs demonstrate the limits the thoughtful researcher placed on himself. The deleted photograph (Figure 4) is the most significant photograph for visual ethics. Although the researcher had consent to photograph the groups he chose not to use it, believing it could harm the two individuals with entwined legs. Rather than relying solely on informed consent, or procedural ethics, as an ethical catch all, the researcher places consent in context. In the final analysis, the researcher was not only governed by procedural ethics but was also driven reflexively by ethics in context.

REC chair's summary

Photography within an ethnographic project invites a method of data collection that is less focused at the outset than some other research methods, such as interviews.

However, sensitivity to the participants (participants by dint of being photographed) remains important, particularly sensitivity in the use of images. Participants may feel even more strongly about the use of personal images than they do about use of their words and ideas. People are not obligated to take part in research but they may well do so, out of generosity and maybe an interest in what research can contribute to society in general terms. They possibly have a much more developed belief in the importance of freedom of expression and, by association, freedom of the press in a democratic society and in the people's right to know.

Rejecting Figure 5 and accepting Figure 6 for publication creates a strong tension for me when both have two young women experiencing strong emotions as the focal point. I can sense how Figure 5 must appeal to an ethnographer, and how constraining a rights framework is in the exercise of this research approach.

There is nothing new about the negative perception that many researchers traditionally hold of RECs in New Zealand, and, no doubt, institutional review boards (IRBs) in other countries. Researchers in academic institutions value their academic freedom. The necessity to get ethics sign-off for their research projects is an understandable irritant, not helped by often cumbersome processes and, sometimes, reviewers who lack the confidence and experience to work within the spirit of ethics regulations and guidelines rather than to the letter. Historically, ethical review systems arose out of shockingly abusive medical experimentation. Today's biomedical model does not suit all the research to which researchers and reviewers attempt to apply it. Fundamentally, however, respect for persons does apply to all research, both within the researcher–participant relationship and the researcher–reviewer relationship. Essentially, researchers are responsible for conducting their research in an ethical manner. Ethical review should be a resource not a watch-dog. Inter-personal communication is critical to a useful review process, as the experience of writing this article has demonstrated.

Researcher's reflection

When I entered the ethics approval process for this visual ethnography I expected turbulence. As the third author has pointed out, the structure of the application did not help matters. Each technique – observation, semi-structured interviews, photovoice, video taping and still picture photography of the event – should have had its own description of access to participants and informed consent. In hindsight, I believe the compressed nature of this project and the very limited data collection period proved to be a cause for consternation. There was indeed a need for a more widespread unpacking of the numerous aspects of the research process. However, the more frustrating aspect for me was the pre-research phase and the necessity to predict and account for all likely scenarios when I knew full well that the unfolding of this (messy) ethnography could not be driven like a square peg into the round hole of the ethics application template. In preparation for the visual research process I quickly became aware of the numerous calls for guidance, consensus and resolution from visual research advocates. This is especially true for visual ethics (Papademas 2004; Wiles et al. 2008). Clearly it is quite a different beast, yet the uniqueness of visual research as part of this project created a timely opportunity for discussion and reflection. The underpinning consideration that has evolved from this conversation has been the issue of consent. Taking a photograph (in this case of young people at a public sporting venue) must align with an appropriate decision-making process that considers the importance and implications of consent. For me it has highlighted the need to explore a far more fluid and eclectic approach to ethics. The crucial component has been dialogue with my REC chair, something that I think researchers and ethicists do not always embrace. I am very aware of the number of ethics applications that ethics committees must process, leaving little time to engage in the type of conversation we have had. There is a need for balance: between external regulation and internal integrity, between what can be addressed before the fact and what evolves in process, between participants' rights and appropriate representation, and between spontaneity and caution. At the fulcrum of the balance process is decision-making. There will be many conversations and decisions ahead for visual methods researchers.

Tentative guidelines for visual ethnography

We offer five tentative guidelines for visual research ethics that have evolved from this conversation. The first highlights how, even in the presence of commercial media operating without any consent process, the researcher must take responsibility for a reflective ethical process. Second, technology and the photographic equipment that is now available to researchers allows them to utilize the power of focus, zoom, depth of field and blur, promoting the minimization of harm. Third, photos of a context such as a sporting event highlight that there is an ethical difference between physicality (Figure 6) and emotion (Figure 5) and the subsequent potential for harm. Students in Figure 5 display more vulnerability and need more protection when an affective depiction is presented. Fourth, consent is only one moment of the ethics process. Deletion of photographs demonstrates that in ethical practice the researcher can and must protect vulnerable subjects. Fifth, we are unsure of the tipping point for individual consent. We know it does not have a quantifiable threshold like 65 persons, nor can it be predicted in procedural ethics or held as rules in the field. Rather the more important lesson from this exercise is the need for a heightened sensitivity toward consent or potential harm in the production and publication phase of the research process.

Notes

1. Word limits do not allow us to discuss photovoice as well as videotaping/photographing.
2. REC has been used throughout rather than IRB.
3. Although we refer to this image for discussion purposes, Figure 4 will not be included in any subsequent publication.

References

Allen, L. 2009. 'Caught in the act': Ethics committee review and researching the sexual culture of schools. *Qualitative Research* 9: 395–410.

Guillemin, M., and L. Gillam. 2004. Ethics, reflexivity and 'ethically important moments' in research. *Qualitative Inquiry* 10, no. 2: 261–80.

Harper, D. 2005. What's new visually? In *The Sage handbook of qualitative research* 3rd ed., ed. N.K. Denzin and Y. Lincoln, 747–62. Thousand Oaks, CA: Sage.

Papademas, D. 2004. Editor's introduction: Ethics in visual research. *Visual Studies* 19, no. 2: 122–5.

Pink, S. 2007. *Doing visual ethnography*. 2nd ed. London: Sage.

Prosser, J. 1992. Personal reflections on the use of photography in an ethnographic case study. *British Educational Research Journal* 18, no. 4: 397–413.

Prosser, J. 2000. The moral maze of image ethics. In *Situated ethics in educational research*, ed. H. Simons and J. Prosser, 116–32. London: Routledge.

Prosser, J. 2007. Visual methods and the visual culture of schools. *Visual Studies* 22, no. 1: 13–30.

Tolich, M. 2004. Internal confidentiality: When confidentiality assurances fail relational informants. *Qualitative Sociology* 27: 101–6.

Wiles, R., J. Prosser, A. Bagnoli, A. Clark, K. Davies, S. Holland, and E. Renold. 2008. *Visual ethics: Ethical issues in visual research.* Southampton: ESRC National Centre for Research Methods.

Index

Page numbers in *Italics* represent tables.
Page numbers in **Bold** represent figures.